10
PROPHETIC
VALUES
FOR TODAY

10 PROPHETIC VALUES FOR TODAY

HEARING, GLORIFYING AND RESTORING GOD'S VOICE

JAMES LEVESQUE

Chosen
a division of Baker Publishing Group
Minneapolis, Minnesota

Library of Congress Cataloging-in-Publication Data
Names: Levesque, James, author.
Title: 10 prophetic values for today : hearing, glorifying and restoring God's voice / James Levesque.
Other titles: Ten prophetic values for today
Description: Minneapolis, Minnesota : Chosen Books, a division of Baker Publishing Group, [2022] | Includes bibliographical references.
Identifiers: LCCN 2022022337 | ISBN 9780800799342 (trade paper) | ISBN 9780800762902 (casebound) | ISBN 9781493438846 (ebook)
Subjects: LCSH: Values—Religious aspects—Christianity. | Listening—Religious aspects—Christianity. | God (Christianity)
Classification: LCC BJ1275 .L48 2022 | DDC 170—dc23/eng/20220711
LC record available at https://lccn.loc.gov/2022022337

I want to dedicate this book
to the amazing team we have around us
at Engaging Heaven Church.
We have created a culture
of valuing the Kingdom and the prophetic.
If not for all the pastors,
staff and leaders around us,
my wife and I wouldn't be able to do
what we are called to do around the earth.
We love you all. I'm amazed
at what the Lord has started, and the
greatest days are ahead.

CONTENTS

FOREWORD

The Bible is God's written Word. I call it Jesus in Print. But being committed to His written Word doesn't replace my responsibility to hear His voice. Nor can my responsibility to hear His voice ever take the place of my devotion to read and study the Scriptures. They are so intertwined that we must have both to succeed. His Word enables us to hear His voice.

The Word of God is the most powerful thing in the universe. He spoke the universe into being. He separated day from night with a word. He speaks and our reality gets redefined. What is impossible in one moment becomes possible in the next, simply because He declares it so. He is the Word. In Luke 4:4, Jesus quotes this verse out of the Old Testament: "Man shall not live by bread alone, but by every word of God" (NKJV). We are alive because He speaks. Our life in Christ is an evidence of His voice. He has woven into our physical and spiritual design the ability to sense Him, to commune with Him and to hear His voice.

The challenge for our walk of faith is not our inability to hear God's voice but our willingness to listen to other voices and entertain ideas that contradict God's promises to us. Giving audience to other thoughts and ideas empowers those seeds to strangle the Word of God. The Word of God has been planted in us. But we have influence over the outcome.

The sobering reality is Jesus' warning that our traditions make the Word of God powerless.

We manage the soil of our own hearts, stewarding and protecting our connection to His voice—that which gives us life. James Levesque has written significantly on this topic in his new book, *10 Prophetic Values for Today*. These chapters promote a value for the prophetic and guide us to manage our hearts to become a welcome resting place for His voice, which is a manifestation of His presence.

Hebrews 5:14 talks about "those who by reason of use have their senses exercised to discern both good and evil." When people in the banking system are trained to identify counterfeit money, they don't study counterfeit bills. They only study real currency. They become so exposed to the texture, the design of both the front and back of the bill, the character of the font and the weight of the paper that a counterfeit always stands out. We are called to become so intimately immersed in the personhood of God—becoming more and more like Jesus—that we can easily distinguish His voice, His heart and His goodness from anything else. It's an immersion in His presence.

With so many voices swirling around us in this moment in time, this book is vital to the process of every believer as we grow in our discernment of what is true. James writes beautifully about integrity, generosity, community and keeping Jesus as our priority. In these pages, you are receiving not only sound teaching, but also a father's guidance into developing the kind of inner world that will steward well the voice and presence of God. We have been given the greatest gift in the history of humanity—the Holy Spirit resting in and upon us. We must learn to host Him well for our sake and for the sake of the world.

Bill Johnson, Bethel Church, Redding, California; author, *Open Heavens* and *Born for Significance*

ACKNOWLEDGMENTS

Thank you, Brooke Ritson, for your help with this project. You and Richard are such a gift to our lives, and we are thankful we are called to expand the Kingdom together!

1

A HEARING HEART

The Importance of Hearing God's Voice

What a day we live in. There is no doubt that the past few years, even the past decade, have brought us to this place. Are we living in the end times? No doubt. Are we being shaken and prepared for another Great Awakening? Also no doubt. We are living in a "great and dreadful day" (Malachi 4:5). For some of us, there is incredible breakthrough, healing and provision. For others? Lots of confusion and trials. I believe this book is crucial for you as you enter the days ahead. God has visited me and has clearly confirmed what His Word says about the end times. It's good. We win! However, what we do *now* will determine where we go. I believe this final hour will be the greatest hour you and I have ever known in God. Families will be restored, healed and saved. Regions will be transformed. Nations will experience the glory of God like never before. Yet this will all come at a cost.

In the past few years, we have seen so much shaking, so many trials and unforeseen persecution. We have seen the prophetic ministry begin to collapse and then appear to be on life support. On many levels, hearing God has been replaced by attention-seeking prophets who built online kingdoms, only to see them fall. False prophecies mounted and left many people discouraged and even feeling defeated.

In December 2020, as I was praying, I saw a vision of the earth. It was dark. Then I heard a voice out of heaven speak. It wasn't a word, but a sound that looked almost like gold smoke. Immediately, it covered the earth. Then God spoke so clearly to me and said, *I will restore My voice on the earth.*

Of course, I knew His voice had never left, but I also knew that what He said had to do with true prophetic ministry becoming pure again, and God's people hearing Him clearly for themselves. Then the Lord said, *If you keep My voice close, I will protect you and give you discernment through every season of life.*

I grabbed a notepad and began to write 10 prophetic values that, as a pastor, I have observed are missing in people's lives. In my life, I knew that the key to hearing God's voice was not some angelic visitation, or a high-intensity heavenly encounter, but rather a coming back to the foundations of faith—to the message of the Gospel that works. That is what will help us restore our hearing, especially when we combine it with the 10 prophetic values that we will talk about in these pages. We will cover one of these prophetic values in each of the next ten chapters, but let me list them for you here:

1. The value of integrity
2. The value of priority
3. The value of perseverance
4. The value of emotional health

5. The value of relationships
6. The value of loving the written Word of God
7. The value of endless hope
8. The value of knowing what we've been given
9. The value of our speech
10. The value of generosity

When we put these 10 values into practice, they will help us listen to and glorify God's voice the way we must in this day we live in.

Everything Begins with a Word

As we read the Bible, we realize it starts with a word. Literally.

> In the beginning God created the heavens and the earth. Now the earth was formless and empty, darkness was over the surface of the deep, and the Spirit of God was hovering over the waters.
> And God said, "Let there be light," and there was light. God saw that the light was good, and he separated the light from the darkness. God called the light "day," and the darkness he called "night." And there was evening, and there was morning—the first day.
>
> Genesis 1:1–5

Think about that. This earth was framed and formed by God's voice. He spoke; it was. There is a creative power that has been given to us through His voice. When you think of miracles, signs and wonders, it is creation. We speak; it is! That same creative power is in us and is available to us through the hearing of God's voice.

The Bible puts it this way:

> In the beginning was the Word, and the Word was with God, and the Word was God. He was with God in the beginning. Through him all things were made; without him nothing was made that has been made. In him was life, and that life was the light of all mankind. The light shines in the darkness, and the darkness has not overcome it.
>
> John 1:1–5

The Word is God! The Word was there when He spoke. We use that Word as a compass in our lives. This world was created with God's voice, and it is sustained through "the Word," Jesus. As we lean into His voice, we will be directed to walk in power and victory, and we will create . . . again! We will see heaven on earth.

Tighten the Load

One of the words God has been speaking to me lately, and to our church, is to "tighten the load."

Truckers travel far and wide to bring goods and services to many towns and cities. On the major highways of America, you will see truck stops or exits just for truckers to rest and sleep. It is very common, if they are traveling far with goods, for them to pull over and tighten the load. After a long journey, they want to ensure that what they are transporting is secure and safe. I believe this is a moment in time for us as believers to "tighten the load." We must come back to the truths that have shaped this world for God.

The road map to hearing, restoring and glorifying God's voice begins with a desire to hear. A deep longing to know Him and His Word. The Bible's book of Romans says, "So then faith comes by hearing, and hearing by the word of

God" (Romans 10:17 NKJV). Faith comes by hearing! Hearing brings faith. Hearing . . . by the Word of God! Listening to God's voice, through His Word, will bring faith. We will continually walk in victory and power if we listen. Faith is anchored in the unseen realm and is conceived through hearing.

In 1 Corinthians, the apostle Paul wrote about the gifts of the Spirit. He laid out each gift and described its function and operations (see 1 Corinthians 12). Thank God he did that; we now understand the operations of the gifts of the Spirit because of it. And then, after laying out all the gifts, Paul immediately tells us, "It is good that you are enthusiastic and passionate about spiritual gifts, especially prophecy" (1 Corinthians 14:1 TPT).

Why did Paul add that? Were the descriptions not enough? Apparently not. And it makes sense. Knowing about the gifts is not enough. Hearing about their existence is not enough. We must pursue them! What we hunger and thirst for, we will experience.

Why Prophecy?

Out of all the gifts that Paul mentions, why is the gift of prophecy "especially" mentioned? I have often wondered that myself. Quite simply, prophecy is what? Hearing God. There are many situations in which we will need to hear God's voice, and many different people who will be blessed by it. But at the core of it, prophecy is hearing God Himself. Paul explains that we must desire all the gifts, but we especially need to desire to hear God. That is the realm of faith. That is the gift by which every gift flows. Through relationship, we hear our Father and walk in His ways.

One thing I've realized these past few years is that God's voice is our anchor. When people are confused, we have His voice. When people are wondering what's next, His voice calms us and directs us. I don't have confidence in much, but I know the voice of the Lord will guide us like the cloud in the wilderness (see Exodus 13:21–22).

Hearing God's voice will always require spending time in His Word, praying and being with Him. Living in God's presence and valuing His voice will lead to a transformation of our lives. I know when God is speaking. I have spent years learning to hear Him. I also know when to tell people what He is saying or not saying. When you hear God's voice, He may speak some specific things to you, but not all those things are necessarily to be shared. Some may just be for you to pray about.

Romans 12:6 challenges us to prophesy according to our faith. It is easy to get caught up in the end-of-the-world, doomsday prophecies. I will tell you to run from that. If we declare only judgment and destruction, we have not spent that much time with Jesus or His Word. And for some, "according to their faith" isn't that great a faith.

We win. Therefore, we must act as though we win. Destruction and evil only continue when the Church remains silent. If we do nothing, things will continue this way. We are the light of the world and the salt of the earth. It's time we start being the seasoning in this earth that God has required us to be.

What Are You Asking For?

I have always been amazed by the encounter Solomon had with God in 1 Kings 3:1–15:

> Solomon made an alliance with Pharaoh king of Egypt and married his daughter. He brought her to the City of

David until he finished building his palace and the temple of the LORD, and the wall around Jerusalem. The people, however, were still sacrificing at the high places, because a temple had not yet been built for the Name of the LORD. Solomon showed his love for the LORD by walking according to the instructions given him by his father David, except that he offered sacrifices and burned incense on the high places.

The king went to Gibeon to offer sacrifices, for that was the most important high place, and Solomon offered a thousand burnt offerings on that altar. At Gibeon the LORD appeared to Solomon during the night in a dream, and God said, "Ask for whatever you want me to give you."

Solomon answered, "You have shown great kindness to your servant, my father David, because he was faithful to you and righteous and upright in heart. You have continued this great kindness to him and have given him a son to sit on his throne this very day.

"Now, LORD my God, you have made your servant king in place of my father David. But I am only a little child and do not know how to carry out my duties. Your servant is here among the people you have chosen, a great people, too numerous to count or number. So give your servant a discerning heart to govern your people and to distinguish between right and wrong. For who is able to govern this great people of yours?"

The Lord was pleased that Solomon had asked for this. So God said to him, "Since you have asked for this and not for long life or wealth for yourself, nor have asked for the death of your enemies but for discernment in administering justice, I will do what you have asked. I will give you a wise and discerning heart, so that there will never have been anyone like you, nor will there ever be. Moreover, I will give you what you have not asked for—both wealth and honor—so that in your lifetime you will have no equal among kings.

And if you walk in obedience to me and keep my decrees and commands as David your father did, I will give you a long life." Then Solomon awoke—and he realized it had been a dream.

He returned to Jerusalem, stood before the ark of the Lord's covenant and sacrificed burnt offerings and fellowship offerings. Then he gave a feast for all his court.

Solomon could have asked for anything. God was willing to grant him whatever he wanted. In the midst of this encounter, however, he asked for a "discerning heart," which is also translated as a "hearing heart."[1] Solomon asked for a heart to hear. He wanted above all else to hear clearly and discern properly. I love the Lord's response to Solomon. Because Solomon didn't ask for selfish things, God said He would give him wisdom. Wisdom comes from hearing God.

I was with a very well-known older prophet years ago. He looked at me and said, "You know what will be the greatest gift in the final hour?"

I was taken aback and replied, "No, I don't . . . miracles?"

"No," he said. "Long after I'm gone, remember this conversation. The greatest gift will be the gift of discernment."

I was shocked. I was fairly young, and I struggled to understand that concept. *Surely wisdom is important*, I thought, *and I know about the teachings of discernment in the Bible, but discernment? Really?*

I just couldn't see it at the time. I was convinced that the greatest gift had to be miracles or even faith. I believed this wise prophet, but it would be many years until I understood more fully what he had told me.

Today, I am floored at the lack of discernment in the Body of Christ. People who have walked with God for years as generals are finding themselves confused and are declaring things that are not even biblical. Presidents, seasons, COVID-19— dealing with all these things requires proper discernment, and so many people are struggling to make sense of what God is saying. When we long to hear His voice and, like Solomon, ask for "a hearing heart" to discern, there will be no confusion. When we long to hear His voice, there will be clarity and complete victory.

What Are You Declaring?

Ask, seek and knock. One thing we will talk about ahead is the power of God's Word. If prophecy is speaking God's future words, then we have to understand that what we declare, we will walk in. I believe that so many people are trapped and entangled not because of the devil, but because of their words. The Bible tells us in the book of Proverbs, "Your words are so powerful that they will kill or give life, and the talkative person will reap the consequences" (Proverbs 18:21 TPT).

Our words—what we say, what we declare—such power is in our words! Declaration is not only life but also death. (We will look at the power of words more closely in chapter 10, where we talk about our speech being one of the ten important prophetic values I mentioned at the start.) I have been pastoring a long time, and I know many people who are trapped by their own words—not the devil's. When you say, "I am broke," you will be. When you say, "All men are dogs," they will be. When you say, "No one understands me," we won't.

It is not some hocus-pocus, magic garbage. We frame our world by our words. God does the same. What we say matters. What we are declaring matters. Every day when I take my kids to school, I have them say a declaration. Every single day, they say,

I am a leader, not a follower,
I am the head and not the tail,
I am above and not beneath,
I am a lender, not the borrower,
I am blessed and highly favored,
And I'm going to change this world!

My two-year-old now declares this daily. And every day, as we declare this over our lives, my kids begin to believe it. They start to walk in the confidence and power of being a child of God. The world out there all day long will tell you the opposite about yourself. The online world is filled with images and words that want to trap you in comparison and jealousy.

I pray today that you will resolve to speak only life. I pray today that you get a revelation of who you are as God's child, and a revelation of the authority you have been given. As we begin to declare God's Word, we will realize what we have been given and walk in that!

We Must Hear His Voice

Do you long to hear God's voice on a daily basis? Do you need wisdom in this hour more than ever before? Chances are that you answered yes to both questions. Just as we learned from Solomon, hearing and wisdom are intertwined. If you want to walk in wisdom and revelation, you have to hear God's voice for daily direction. Just like Solomon, we must ask for a hearing heart.

A few years ago, my family and I traveled to France, a beautiful place we have visited and ministered in before. This time, our ultimate purpose was to take a cruise. This was our tenth wedding anniversary, and Debbie and I were planning on cruising around Spain and Africa for our celebration. We could hardly wait!

Our kids and some of our extended family were with us, and it was going to be an awesome time. We landed in Paris, and planned to fly from Paris to Nice, in the south of France. We would be in France for only a day, because we shortly had to get to Spain, from where the cruise would depart. We hadn't been to Nice before, and as a gift, my mother-in-law had a private driver and tour guide ready to pick us up. We would take a mini sight-seeing tour on a private boat, and much more. Our reservations were already in place.

As we all waited in the terminal to board the plane for Nice, I could hear the anticipation and excitement in my family members' voices as they conversed about the day ahead. All of a sudden, the room became silent to me. I heard the Lord clearly say to me, *Don't get on that plane!*

I was shocked. Then I heard it again: *Don't get on that plane!*

What was I supposed to do? I didn't really understand why I was hearing His voice. As my stomach began to feel sick, I realized that I needed to say something. But our bags were on the plane, we had boarding passes in hand, and to make it a more difficult experience, I heard the attendant say over the loudspeaker, "Now boarding group one."

I quickly ran up to the desk. "Excuse me," I said, "we aren't going on that flight."

The airline employee told me, "That's not possible; it's too late to change flights."

After I made it very clear that we weren't flying and that she needed to get our bags off the plane, she relented and called a supervisor. Thankfully, I have a wife who knows how to listen and yield to the voice of God. Without hesitation, Debbie told the supervisor, "Well, we aren't getting on the flight!"

I apologized to our family. I didn't have an explanation, other than that I knew we weren't supposed to get on that flight. After literally hours at the airport, waiting for bags and trying to figure out what we would do next, we decided to go to a nearby hotel and wait for a flight that would be leaving for Spain a few days later. I still did not know why the Lord had told us not to go to Nice, yet I was walking in the peace of being obedient.

Later that night, as we were getting ready for bed, a news alert came up on my phone. It was about Air France. I was stunned, and immediately I turned on the TV at the hotel. The news said a company-wide strike was happening with the airline. Never had such a thing happened on that level before in France, so no one had expected this. The airline announced that there would be no other Air France flights in the foreseeable future.

As I watched the screen, it hit me—we would not have been able to come back for our cruise. If we had gotten on that flight, we would have missed our anniversary trip, which would have been devastating. (Our upcoming flight to Spain was on a different airline.)

I was relieved and thankful. Imagine God caring so much about our lives that He would speak to me so strongly, just so we would make our flight to Spain for the cruise! I was so moved by this. Not for my sake; I just couldn't help but think about the possibilities when we hear God's voice clearly. Later that night, as I was lying in bed about to go to sleep,

I heard the Lord again. He said, *We are entering the days when every move must be with My Word.*

I am telling you today, we have to have a desire to hear God. Not for silly things like a vacation, but for our real navigation of the end times. Every week, someone says to me, "We're living in ever-changing times." Although that may be true for you, there is one thing that does not change. Our Bible says, "Jesus, the Anointed One, is always the same—yesterday, today, and forever" (Hebrews 13:8 TPT). Wherever we are going, His voice must be our guide. His Word must be our lamp. I believe that if we will desire His voice and lean into Him in this hour, there will be no confusion. Will you commit yourself to desiring His Word? Will you resolve to declare life? His voice is what matters. That's it. His words, His Word.

The past few years have felt like the old *Left Behind* movies. Countless decisions to make, and countless opportunities for distraction. God's voice is the only thing that has sustained me. I would say that 2020 was one of the most extraordinary years in our world history. Economic collapses, a worldwide pandemic, the world being shut down. Even as I write this later, most people I know are still recovering from an event that happened a couple of years ago!

Yet 2020 was one of the greatest years we have ever had, both personally and as a church. We declared it from the beginning. We expanded into Florida in December 2020. We purchased a church building in Madeira Beach during a time when many churches were closing or were shut down. All because we believed. We believed God's words, we declared them, we stood on them. He hasn't changed, and neither have His words.

Prophetic Declaration and Prayer

I prophesy this to you today: If you begin to desire the Lord's voice and come back to the values I will list in these pages, your life will be transformed beyond anything you would ever imagine. On every level, in every way.

God is waiting for all of us to honor and value His voice again.

Speak, Lord, for Your servants are listening.

Powerful Points about Prophetic Values

- God spoke so clearly to me and said, *I will restore My voice on the earth.* Of course, God's voice has never left, but what He said had to do with true prophetic ministry becoming pure again, and God's people hearing Him clearly for themselves.

- The Lord also said, *If you keep My voice close, I will protect you and give you discernment through every season of life.*

- The key to hearing God's voice is in coming back to the foundations of faith—to the message of the Gospel that works. That is what will help us restore our hearing, especially when we combine it with the 10 prophetic values in this book.

- When we put the 10 prophetic values I will talk about into practice, they will help us listen to and glorify God's voice. Here they are in a list: the value of integrity, the value of priority, the value of perseverance, the value of emotional health, the value of relationships, the value of loving the written Word of God, the value of endless hope, the value of knowing what we've been given, the value of our speech, and the value of our generosity.

- Everything begins with a word. This earth was framed and formed by God's voice. He spoke; it was. Miracles, signs and wonders work the same way. We speak; it is! That same creative power is in us and is available to us through the hearing of His voice.

- This is a moment in time for us as believers to "tighten the load," as truckers do over a long haul of goods. We must come back to the truths that have shaped this world for God, especially the truths about gifts of the Spirit such as prophecy.

- At the core of it, prophecy is hearing God Himself. The apostle Paul explained that we must desire all the gifts, but that we especially need to desire hearing God.

- One thing I've realized is that God's voice is our anchor. When people are confused, we have His voice. When people are wondering what's next, His voice calms us and directs us.

- Dealing with life requires proper discernment. When we long to hear God's voice and, like Solomon, we ask for "a hearing heart" to discern, there will be no confusion. Instead, there will be clarity and complete victory.

- We frame our world by our words. God does the same. What we say matters. What we are declaring matters. We need to resolve to speak only life.

- As the Lord also spoke to me, *We are entering the days when every move must be with My Word.*

- "Jesus, the Anointed One, is always the same—yesterday, today, and forever" (Hebrews 13:8 TPT). Where we are going, His voice must be our guide. His Word must be our lamp. His voice is what matters. That's it. His words, His Word.

2

PURE CHILDREN OF GOD

The Value of Integrity

Ahh . . . living clean.

At this point, if you've walked with God for a few years, I'm sure you've been a victim of dead religion. If you haven't, praise the Lord, you are a rare breed. Many of us became born again in "Spirit-filled" churches, only to think revival was a repent-a-thon. A constant reminder of how we haven't been close to God. Dead religion will never get you close to God. Feeling horrible about yourself is not the key to anything.

On the other hand, what began with love, grace and mercy sometimes turns into somewhat of an "anything goes" Christianity. Yes, love always wins, but the Bible says this:

> Do the riches of his extraordinary kindness make you take him for granted and despise him? Haven't you experienced how kind and understanding he has been to you? Don't

mistake his tolerance for acceptance. Do you realize that all the wealth of his extravagant kindness is meant to melt your heart and lead you into repentance?

Romans 2:4–6 TPT

The kindness and love of God are essential for our walk with Him, and will even lead us into repentance. Yet changing our lives into His image has to be a result of right living.

Easter is always a wild time for a pastor. You never know who will show up and what kind of wild conversations you will end up having. Last Easter, a guest walked up to me right after church and said, "Can I ask you a question?"

"Sure," I replied. "What's up?"

"Do you believe you can lose your salvation? Because I don't!" he shared with great passion.

I am always amused by people's angles and reactions. "If you're saved, you're saved," I replied. "However, if you're born again, your relationship with sin must change."

I realize that the people asking that question are usually not living right and are trying to see how much they can get away with. If we are walking in the light and living clean, those questions don't happen. People who will go to hell are not living for God, whether they knew Him at one time or not. We have to realize that there is a place of communion with God and a holiness that will empower us to overcome in these last days.

Purity in Prophecy

I remember many years ago being in Rhode Island. A certain nationally known prophet was coming to town, and the host pastor asked me if I would be willing to attend for a night. I told him I would come. When I arrived, the prophet was in the back room, and I was invited to come back and meet him. He was from South Africa, so I wasn't sure if I would have the opportunity again.

I had known who he was for a long time. I was even greatly blessed by his ministry. I had heard of some really accurate prophesies he had spoken that had come to pass. On the other hand, there was a great list of prophetic words he had spoken that didn't, or at least had not yet come to pass. Some had timelines and hadn't happened. Needless to say, I was still thankful to get to spend time with him.

When I was introduced to him, I instantly felt God's presence, a sign to me of his love for God. He knew about our ministry in New England, and we chatted a little about that. We talked about some things God had given him, and just generally what he was feeling the Lord had to say for New England. I did notice that he seemed very tired. Maybe even a little worn out. As we were wrapping up our conversation because the service was about to start, I asked him a question: "Is there anything I can pray for you about?" I was hoping to be an encouragement to him.

"Yes, young man," he quickly replied. "I need strength."

He began to tell me how difficult and weary prophetic ministry was. And then he began to "pull back the curtain" and share some challenges with his ministry. To be honest, I have seen this happen with many of my heroes of the faith. I have met so many, and I am always so grateful for that. It's always an honor. I even tell you this story knowing that this prophet was a great man of God.

He began to tell me that in the early days, he had not felt pressured to deliver prophetic words. When he heard from God clearly, he would deliver the word and it would come to pass. There were no crowds or *The Elijah List* or other online publications. It was God and this prophet. He felt this

was the purest time in his ministry. Fast-forward to now—
there was a "pressure," as he called it, to deliver a powerful
prophetic word to each crowd, even if he "didn't have one."

As a result, he has delivered prophecies in moments, and
on big stages, that simply were not from God. As he looked
back on many years of his ministry, I could see that this discouraged him. He pleaded with me to "keep the flow pure."
And he urged that as God promoted our lives and ministry,
we should not forget what we did at first.

It would be ten years later before it happened again. This
time I was in California, and meeting with an amazing healing evangelist. This man had been my hero in the faith when
I was a new believer. I attended about seven of his crusades,
sometimes waiting outside for seven hours to get in. And
here I was, seeing a tired man of God, still so powerful and
anointed, yet pretty discouraged, pleading with me not to
lose trust with God and the anointing.

"The Holy Spirit is the most precious person we have,"
this evangelist told me.

Both these experiences really impacted me. I knew I wanted
to stay pure. I didn't want money, crowds or fame to take away
the gifts God had given me. I have found myself on many
occasions on the front lines of some major moves of God.
Some of my best friends have led, and some lead to this day,
some of the greatest moves of God on this earth. Likewise,
we continue to see God awaken cities and regions. Signs,
wonders and miracles follow every meeting. But above all, I
want to stay clean.

Ultimately, purity allows us to see God continually. As
Matthew 5:8–10 (TPT) tells us,

What bliss you experience when your heart is pure! For then
your eyes will open to see more and more of God.

How joyful you are when you make peace! For then you will be recognized as a true child of God.

How enriched you are when persecuted for doing what is right! For then you experience the realm of heaven's kingdom.

⬤ Presidential Elections

It was 2004 when Senator Barack Obama appeared on *The Oprah Winfrey Show*. I didn't realize it at the time, but this was months before Obama would give a speech at the Democratic National Convention. He was appearing in one of his first national interviews on a big scale. My mom would always watch Oprah, whose widely popular talk show came on every afternoon. One day when I walked in to visit with Mom, I was talking to her and briefly saw that Oprah was on—nothing out of the ordinary. At second glance, I saw this African American politician on the screen with his wife, and as I turned around to walk away, I heard the Lord speak so clearly: *He will be the next U.S. president.*

I was floored. *Clearly, I am not hearing this right*, I thought. *Why would God tell me? I am nobody. Could this be God?*

I dismissed it, finished chatting with my mom and went to get a drink. When I passed the TV again, I heard the Lord a second time: *This man will be the next president of the United States.*

Now I was convinced that he would be president. I asked my mom if she knew who he was, and she said no. I wrote his name down and brought it to our prayer team. In fact, I went to everyone I knew and told them. I had so many people tell me that I wasn't hearing from God—mostly Republicans! Although Obama was four years away from possibly running, I told everyone I could trust—pastors and leaders, spiritual fathers. I told them I wasn't sure why

God was telling me, but that we needed to pray and to be prepared.

In 2008, four years after I heard that prophetic word, in historic fashion Barack Obama won:

> Obama won a decisive victory over McCain, winning the Electoral College and the popular vote by a sizable margin, including states that had not voted for the Democratic presidential candidate since 1976 (North Carolina) and 1964 (Indiana and Virginia). Obama received the largest share of the popular vote won by a Democrat since Lyndon B. Johnson in 1964 and was the first Democrat to win an outright majority of the popular vote since Jimmy Carter in 1976. Obama's total count of 69.5 million votes stood as the largest tally ever won by a presidential candidate until 2020.[1]

When this happened, many of our prayer leaders repented for coming against the word I believe God had told me, and some pastors felt encouraged about the possibility of hearing God for future life-changing events. I wasn't sure about all of that, but I was grateful that at 24 years old I had begun to hear God so clearly.

Immediately after Obama became president, people started asking me who the next president would be. I thought this was bizarre and awkward, but I understood people's desire to know. I would even be ministering at churches and people would ask who the next president of the United States would be. I would quickly respond, "God hasn't told me."

First Corinthians 13:9 (NLT) tells us, "Now our knowledge is partial and incomplete, and even the gift of prophecy reveals only part of the whole picture!" We only know part. Part. God only reveals part. That means we should not try to force the "parts" that we don't know.

I remember being in a prophetic conference where we were doing a panel discussion for the crowd. Someone asked, "Who did God tell you the next president of the United States will be?"

"God didn't," I said. "I never know. This wasn't meant to be a yearly thing." Meaning, I am not a robot who can predict election results.

Over the years, many prophetic ministers both young and old have fallen into this trap. One might say, "Trump will win his reelection, says the Lord." Then another minister might see that word and tag on, "The Lord says that Donald Trump will win by a landslide," and so on. Not only does the ministers' credibility get ruined; the prophetic ministry in general also gets set back. People get skeptical and feel that much of the prophetic is a circus and is flaky.

God has not stopped speaking, however, and we must position ourselves to hear the clear word of God continually! I believe that integrity in life, not just in the prophetic, is the key to honoring God's voice and seeing it restored on the earth. Let's take a deeper look into integrity.

Living with Integrity, Like Job

We must understand the power of integrity. One definition of integrity is "the quality of being honest and having strong moral principles."[2] There are some amazing Scriptures on integrity. Proverbs 10:9 (ESV) says, "Whoever walks in integrity walks securely, but he who makes his ways crooked will be found out." Proverbs 28:6–8 (TPT) says,

> It's more respectable to be poor and pure than rich and perverse.

To be obedient to what you've been taught proves you're an honorable child, but to socialize with the lawless brings shame to your parents.

Go ahead and get rich on the backs of the poor, but all the wealth you gather will one day be given to those who are kind to the needy.

Job was a man of integrity. Job 1:1 says, "In the land of Uz there lived a man whose name was Job. This man was blameless and upright; he feared God and shunned evil." Job was blameless. He had integrity. Integrity is the currency of influence. If the gifts of the Spirit were paper money, integrity would be the gold backing them. A lack of integrity in our lives is like a clogged pipe; the Word of God cannot flow freely.

Looking at the story of Job, we can learn a lot about walking in integrity. Integrity is silent. It is who you are when no one is around. It is the currency of this life. As followers of Christ, we must long to walk in purity and have our hearts clean before God. This affects how we hear. Integrity will be a riverbank for the prophetic ministry.

As we examine the life of Job, we see four areas that he walked clean in, areas that will help us live "blameless" lives. Let's take a look at these four primary areas I believe God wants us to walk in, like Job.

1. Integrity in the area of fearing God

As we just read, Job "feared God." God wants us to live with a fear of Him. This isn't a demonic fear, but a holy fear, knowing that He is holy, and that He commands us to live holy lives. Also, fearing God takes an inner strength to turn away from temptation and say no to the things in this life that separate us from God, including sin.

Proverbs 1:7 tells us, "The fear of the LORD is the beginning of knowledge, but fools despise wisdom and instruction." Fearing God opens the door for knowledge, and wisdom will flow through that. Wise men and women are people who fear God.

2. Financial integrity

The Bible says Job was the wealthiest man in the east (see Job 1:3). This is a big one. Part of Job's walking blameless was in the realm of financial integrity.

How do you handle large sums of money? How do you share and give your overflow? How honest are you, even when it doesn't benefit you? A brother in Christ once called me and said, "Someone forgot to scan one of my items at Walmart." He was almost testifying that he had gotten a free item he hadn't paid for. Then a day later, as my wife was unloading her cart into the car, she noticed one item that hadn't been scanned. Although we were in a hurry, she went back in and let the store know so we could pay for it.

Trust me, it's the little things in life in the area of money that will hold us back.

3. Integrity with our friends

The Bible says that Job had friends who stood by him (see Job 2:11). This tells us that in the worst time of his life, there were friends who surrounded him and loved him. Simply put, we were not meant to do life alone. We were created to live in covenant relationships and do life together. My heart breaks when I see ministers walk alone, or not live in covenant relationships. Likewise, as you are reading this, open your heart up to love and to living life with others.

Are you quick to resolve conflict? Are you quick to forgive? How we handle our relationships can hold us back and hinder us from hearing the Lord's voice. I have been pastoring for over 25 years, and more often than not, I have seen misunderstandings result in bitterness and unforgiveness in people's lives. You need to have relationships in your life worth honoring and fighting for.

4. Integrity with our family

Job 1:2 tells us that Job had seven sons and three daughters. His integrity was extended to his family. Family is tricky sometimes. We don't get to choose them; we are given them. Yet we are commanded to honor them. I thank God for fathers like Job, men of God who walk blameless, full of integrity. When you walk this way, it will flow down to your children. We have an obligation to love our families and pass down to them the example of our integrity.

Integrity is about stewardship. Stewarding our relationship with God, our finances, friends and family. As we are faithful in these areas that God has given us, increase will flow in our lives, including greater measures of hearing His voice.

Eyes on Jesus

Hebrews 12:2 says we should be "fixing our eyes on Jesus, the pioneer and perfecter of faith. For the joy set before him he endured the cross, scorning its shame, and sat down at the right hand of the throne of God." Integrity is about fixing our eyes on Jesus.

When King Jehoshaphat was in the midst of an ugly war, he called an assembly and declared, "Our God, will you not judge them? For we have no power to face this vast army that is attacking us. We do not know what to do, but our eyes are on you" (2 Chronicles 20:12).

Whom are your eyes on? Are they on Jesus? What we behold, we become. If we are looking to Jesus, He will be the reward. If we are looking to other people or to our circumstances, we will fail to walk in purity and integrity, and ultimately we will hinder the flow of God's voice.

There is a celebrity culture in Christianity that has taken away the image of Jesus. As ministers, we must always point to Jesus, making a path for others to follow. Paul declared in 1 Corinthians 11:1, "Follow my example, as I follow the example of Christ."

We are all following Christ, and, thankfully, pure men and women of God pave the way. But we must not worship the men and women who lead us.

That also means when people fall, we don't kick them either. The men and women who have given incorrect prophetic words or have even prophesied election results incorrectly are only human, and one false prophecy doesn't discredit many years of valid ministry. I believe this is a vital principle in cleansing our hearts to hear the voice of God. You and I were wired to hear His voice; He created us to hear Him.

I was blown away in 2020, after the presidential election in America, at how many people got discouraged and even walked away from prophetic ministry. I'm sure some people were sad about the election results, but the greater disappointment had to do with "prophets" who missed hearing God. Many did.

Let me be clear: I do not think many of these people were prophets. Some of them needed to be exposed and humbled. Yet I also have friends who honestly missed God at the time, giving a false prophecy. It doesn't take away from their credibility at all.

If our focus is Jesus, and not a politician or a Facebook prophet, we won't be discouraged when things don't work out as we had hoped. Jesus will never let us down. As long as our eyes are on Him, we will be seated in the right place. Realize that God has given you the same access to Him as any person out there. Learn to listen to Him. He will speak clearly and direct your paths.

Prophetic Declaration and Prayer

I declare over you today that from this day forward, you will hear God's voice more clearly than ever before, and that your eyes will remain on Him! Join me in this prayer:

Lord, we thank You for all that You have given us— our family, our friends and all of our provision. I pray today that we would value integrity highly and walk in purity as we become stewards of all You have given to us. I thank You that in the days ahead, it will be said of us that like Job, we are "blameless" and we "fear God." We commit all of this to You today, in Jesus' mighty name. Amen.

Powerful Points about the Prophetic

- The kindness and love of God are essential for our walk with Him, and will even lead us into repentance. Yet changing our lives into His image has to be a result of right living.
- We have to realize that there is a place of communion with God and a holiness that will empower us to overcome in these last days.
- Ultimately, purity allows us to see God continually. As Matthew 5:8 (TPT) tells us: "What bliss you experience when your heart is pure! For then your eyes will open to see more and more of God."
- We must position ourselves to hear the clear word of God continually! I believe that valuing integrity in life, not just in the prophetic, is key to honoring God's voice and seeing it restored on the earth.
- Integrity is the currency of influence. If the gifts of the Spirit were paper money, integrity would be the gold backing them.
- A lack of integrity in our lives is like a clogged pipe; the Word of God cannot flow freely.
- As followers of Christ, we must long to walk in purity and have our hearts clean before God. This affects how we hear. Integrity will be a riverbank for the prophetic ministry.
- Job modeled four areas of integrity that we should walk clean in, as he did: integrity in the area of fearing God (knowing He is holy and commands us to live holy lives), financial integrity (in all things, both large and small), integrity with our friends (doing life together with others) and integrity with our family (passing down to them the example of our integrity).

- Integrity is about stewardship. Stewarding our relationship with God, our finances, friends and family. As we are faithful with these areas, increase will flow in our lives, including greater measures of hearing God's voice.
- Integrity is about fixing our eyes on Jesus. What we behold, we become. If we are looking to Jesus, He will be the reward.
- If we are looking to other people or to our circumstances, we will fail to walk in purity and integrity, and ultimately we will hinder the flow of God's voice.
- We must not worship the men and women who lead us. Yet when people fall, we don't kick them either. One false prophecy doesn't discredit many years of valid ministry. This is a vital principle in cleansing our hearts to hear the voice of God. You and I were wired to hear His voice; He created us to hear Him.
- If our focus is Jesus, and not a politician or a Facebook prophet, we won't be discouraged when things don't work out as we had hoped. Jesus will never let us down.
- Realize that God has given you the same access to Him as any person out there. Learn to listen to Him. He will speak clearly and direct your paths.

3

THE DISCIPLINE
TO SAY NO

The Value of Priority

January 9, 2007. It was a day that would change your life and mine forever. Little did we realize the impact of that Tuesday afternoon.

Steve Jobs, the CEO of Apple Computer, Inc., blew our minds that day. He held a small device in his hand. He called it the "iPhone." He told us that the future was here, in a device that not only was a phone but could also take pictures. He also told us we could listen to music on it. That was incredible! He also said in the future we could have GPS on it, and the iPhone would give us turn-by-turn directions when we were traveling. It would be a whole computer in the size and function of a phone. Steve's announcement was wild, and I knew I had to have one.

And yes, he was right. That phone would replace an entire office. The iPhone would allow us to work, call, write documents and do everything in between. Years ago, a pastor would have a home phone (which was hard for people to get the number for), and an office phone, which people could call, and if it was after hours, they could leave a message and hope to get a call back. Now? You can just text your pastor, family and friends, or even those in another country. For sure, the iPhone has revolutionized life as we know it. Look at today's statistics:[1]

- More than half the population is under 30.
- More people have cell phones than toothbrushes.
- Every day, over 20,000 searches occur, looking for something that has never been searched before, expanding our knowledge.
- An average person checks his or her phone every 4 minutes.
- During an average sermon? It's 12 times.
- An average person spends 5 hours a day online (3 hours on social media).
- You will spend an average of 6 years of your life online.
- Teenagers are more addicted, spending 10 hours a day or more on their phones.
- We use our phones for workouts, news, music, emails, shopping, groceries, games and many other apps and functions. Even your old iPhone is 30 times the speed of the navigational computer that sent the Apollo shuttle to the moon!
- Within minutes of waking up, 60 percent of people will check their phone.

- When in bed, 80 percent of people sleep with their phone next to them.
- Now 210 million people admit that they have an addiction to their phone.
- Forget drunk driving—texting while driving is 6 times more likely than alcohol to cause an accident.

So, was it all good? Not really.

Honestly, I love my phone! Probably too much, and likely by the time you are reading this book, these stats will be even more out of control. Just as a prisoner in jail has to live behind and speak through five-inch glass, you may be held prisoner to a small screen. In some ways, today's smartphone has become a weapon of mass distraction and mass destruction.

Paul writes to the church in Corinth something so profound:

> But this I say, brethren, the time is short, so that from now on even those who have wives should be as though they had none, those who weep as though they did not weep, those who rejoice as though they did not rejoice, those who buy as though they did not possess, and those who use this world as not misusing it. For the form of this world is passing away.
>
> But I want you to be without care. He who is unmarried cares for the things of the Lord—how he may please the Lord. But he who is married cares about the things of the world—how he may please his wife. There is a difference between a wife and a virgin. The unmarried woman cares about the things of the Lord, that she may be holy both in body and in spirit. But she who is married cares about the things of the world—how she may please her husband. And this I say for your own profit, not that I may put a leash on

you, but for what is proper, and that you may serve the Lord without distraction.

1 Corinthians 7:29–35 NKJV

Wow. Paul is telling us married people to live as if we are single so we can "serve the Lord without distraction." (Obviously, that doesn't mean we separate, but even in marriage our focus, our first love, has to be the Lord.) What's more incredible is that Paul wrote this almost 2,000 years ago, in AD 53! Yes, you read that right. What did Paul see almost 2,000 years ago that means so much today? What were they distracted with? And why was it so important to serve the Lord without any distractions? Let's look at that kind of question in our own lives.

How Loud Is the World to You?

I remember waking up one morning and hearing the Lord say to me, *If you want to hear My voice, you must turn down the volume of the world!*

I was taken aback at first. It caused me to consider, *How loud is the world to me?* I usually sleep with a sound machine of some sort on. We have traveled to just over seventy nations of the world, and a sound system is essential for my family and me if we are to sleep well. No matter where we are, I can count on that white noise.

I remember a time in Holland when I was sleeping in my hotel with my sound machine on. All of a sudden, my power cord exploded and shut my machine off. It's pretty common when you use an adapter in a foreign country to have the cord short out and fry so it doesn't work. This time, however, it left a burn mark all over the connector. But what was worse for me was the sudden silence. Immediately, I awoke and tried to figure out what to do to make more noise! This sounds crazy, but I actually turned on the TV and covered the screen with a towel, just to get it dark but have some white noise.

In 2020, most of the world went into some sort of lockdown. It seemed ridiculous, but in the name of safety, we all had to quarantine, which meant many people stayed at home and couldn't leave. In that moment, the Internet became people's main source of entertainment. Many Christians were stuck at home, and much like me in my hotel in Holland, they were trying to fill the resulting silence with noise.

Many people found themselves isolated, and the Bible warns us, "A man who isolates himself seeks his own desire; he rages against all wise judgment" (Proverbs 18:1 NKJV). The lockdowns hurt people's judgment and discernment. As a result, our priorities changed. This phone that was such a life-changing blessing began to take away from Jesus as our priority. As a pastor, I noticed three areas of life that suffered the greatest attack during this time: *self-esteem*, *connection with people* and *connection with God*. Take a closer look:

1. Self-Esteem

When you are spending so much time online looking at everyone else's best moments, you can begin to feel bad about your own life. You cannot compare someone else's social media highlight reel to your darkest moments.

2. Connection with People

So many of us are so used to "liking" or "following" friends and family on social media that we fail to value the ones we have in real life. This kind of online connection leads to disconnection. As a result, making our real, in-person connections a priority is one of the major areas that has suffered. The online world has become a fantasy of sorts, causing people to want to escape the amazing lives they have but are not prioritizing. I know people who lost real relationships because they didn't value or prioritize those connections.

3. Connection with God

This has by far been the greatest attack of the enemy in the past few years. You would think that we would listen to the words of Paul and remove any distractions so we can pursue heaven with all we have.

Matthew 6:33 (NKJV) says, "But seek first the kingdom of God and His righteousness, and all these things shall be added to you." Jesus gave us an essential key here about receiving from God: seeking first. As we prioritize heaven, we will hear God's voice clearly and honor it.

God Longs for More of You

I remember in 2008, shortly after we were married, my wife and I were surprised by a move of God's Spirit. At the time, one of my best friends who was a minister did a weekend of meetings, and God moved. The weekend turned into extended meetings and then turned into a stadium crowd nightly. We witnessed thousands of miracles and thousands of people nightly showing up to the meetings. Debbie and I were just helping any way we could, and we were excited to see God move.

It was a wild time for us. We had just gotten married and were traveling every week. At one point, we had our clothes in multiple cities across the country, due to never being in one place. We rented an apartment in Connecticut that we stayed in probably twice in the first seven months. It was awesome. I was traveling and speaking every weekend, and even throughout the week. Yet in the middle of it all, one night when I was at a hotel in Michigan, as I was going to sleep, I heard the Lord say, *I want to spend time with you.*

I couldn't believe it.

I want more of you, I heard Him say again.

That God wanted to spend time with me was not the issue. It was that I was already traveling every week, preaching and doing meetings. I thought, *How could God possibly want more of me when all I feel I'm doing is being with Him?*

Then it dawned on me—sure, I was with Him. But all the meetings I was doing were for others. God wasn't only interested in my outward expression to the Body of Christ. He wanted just *me*.

We can get so busy around Jesus that we fail just to *be*. The Bible says in Psalm 46:10, "Be still, and know that I am God; I will be exalted among the nations, I will be exalted in the earth."

Be. It's that simple.

Be still, and know that I am God.

Be still, and know that I am.

Be still, and know that I.

Be still, and know that.

Be still, and know.

Be still, and.

Be still.

Be.

Sometimes we need just to *be*.

As we realize how distracted we have become, we realize that we aren't *being* the way God desires. And in this world, it's remaining at His feet that will enable us to hear His voice.

What we are prioritizing matters. Allowing His voice to be a priority in our lives will require us to *be* more than *do*.

In the Bible, we see a powerful example of setting priorities through the lives of Mary and Martha:

> As Jesus and his disciples were on their way, he came to a village where a woman named Martha opened her home to him. She had a sister called Mary, who sat at the Lord's feet listening to what he said. But Martha was distracted by all the preparations that had to be made. She came to him and asked, "Lord, don't you care that my sister has left me to do the work by myself? Tell her to help me!"
>
> "Martha, Martha," the Lord answered, "you are worried and upset about many things, but few things are needed—or indeed only one. Mary has chosen what is better, and it will not be taken away from her."
>
> Luke 10:38–42

The approach Jesus took in this unique story is amazing. Here we have two people who love God and are both serving Him. Both Mary and Martha wanted to please Him. Jesus acknowledged how it appeared that many things were needed; however, only one was necessary. There was one thing that Jesus said was needed. Does this mean we shouldn't serve in setup or in preparing a place for Jesus? No. What this means is that you will accomplish more at His feet than anywhere else.

If we are going to hear God's voice clearly, we will have to pass the priority test. In the midst of working, honoring and serving Jesus, we must make sure our service is coming from a place at His feet. From the "better" part, we will accomplish more, with less striving.

In the book of John, we see a similar story of distraction. There was a Samaritan woman at the well whose story you are probably familiar with. When she came to draw water, Jesus asked her, "Will you give me a drink?" (John 4:7). John tells us that the disciples had gone into the town to buy food, which is an important point in the story. When they returned, they were surprised because Jesus was talking to a woman who was also a Samaritan, which was considered doubly dirty. Here's more of the story:

> Just then his disciples returned and were surprised to find him talking with a woman. But no one asked, "What do you want?" or "Why are you talking with her?"
>
> Then, leaving her water jar, the woman went back to the town and said to the people, "Come, see a man who told me everything I ever did. Could this be the Messiah?" They came out of the town and made their way toward him.
>
> Meanwhile his disciples urged him, "Rabbi, eat something."
>
> But he said to them, "I have food to eat that you know nothing about."
>
> Then his disciples said to each other, "Could someone have brought him food?"
>
> "My food," said Jesus, "is to do the will of him who sent me and to finish his work. Don't you have a saying, 'It's still four months until harvest'? I tell you, open your eyes and look at the fields! They are ripe for harvest. Even now the one who reaps draws a wage and harvests a crop for eternal life, so that the sower and the reaper may be glad together. Thus the saying 'One sows and another reaps' is true. I sent you to reap what you have not worked for. Others have done the hard work, and you have reaped the benefits of their labor."
>
> John 4:27–38

The disciples went out to get a meal Jesus didn't ask for. Here we have Jesus, ministering to a woman at the well, and

His disciples are not paying attention to what the Lord is doing. Instead, they are feeding their own desires (hunger) and not focusing on the real food. We can learn a couple of keys from this story that will help us stay focused on God and maintain our priorities.

1. Our own desires will pull us away from Jesus.

The disciples were hungry. That wasn't a sin. However, they were pursuing their own interests, while Jesus clearly was operating through the will of God at the well. We have to become more aware of what Jesus is doing. They could have missed an opportunity.

I remember years ago hearing John Wimber say, "We must see what the Father is doing and bless that!"[2]

What is the Father doing in your life? That's the place you need to focus on and lean into. Good works, although seemingly right, can take us away from what the Father is doing.

2. A distracted life will cause us to miss the harvest.

This may be the biggest takeaway from this encounter. Throughout the whole story, the disciples were getting food, and Jesus was ministering to a woman at the well. There was a whole city attached to this encounter. Think about that. This woman would go on to transform a whole city, and through that the world. Her story is widely known past this Scripture, even today. Some denominations even acknowledge her as the apostle Saint Photine of Samaria. This woman was used to expand the Gospel in powerful ways. And yet, during this historic moment, the disciples were not there.

Jesus makes a powerful statement to His disciples in verse 35: "Don't you have a saying, 'It's still four months until harvest'?" Jesus is explaining that there is a mentality, and even a way of speech, that is hindering their urgency. Then He tells them in the same verse to wake up: "I tell you, open your eyes and look at the fields! They are ripe for harvest."

Jesus is pleading with His disciples to set a right priority so they can hear His voice and partner with Him to expand the Gospel. A distracted life will always take away from that.

● One Thing

In all these stories, it is as if Jesus is leading us toward and longing for us to have one focus. We have many responsibilities, but spiritually, we have only one.

I want you to have one focus; I'll take care of the rest, I can hear the Lord saying.

Imagine that in the midst of your hectic life, all the stress and all the unanswered questions can be clarified with one thing . . .

I have always admired the life of David. He is, in fact, one of the greatest heroes in the Bible. It was said of David's life in Acts 13:36, "Now when David had served God's purpose in his own generation, he fell asleep; he was buried with his ancestors and his body decayed."

What a powerful statement about his life. This means that David had accomplished everything the Father had for him. Why David? What was the main factor in David's life? We find one of the secrets in the book of Psalms when we see David in the midst of battle. People are trying to kill him from every side, and as you can imagine, during the battle he makes a request:

The LORD is my light and my salvation—whom shall I fear?
The LORD is the stronghold of my life—of whom shall I be afraid?

53

When the wicked advance against me to devour me, it is
my enemies and my foes who will stumble and fall. Though
an army besiege me, my heart will not fear; though war break
out against me, even then I will be confident.

One thing I ask from the Lord, this only do I seek: that I
may dwell in the house of the Lord all the days of my life, to
gaze on the beauty of the Lord and to seek him in his temple.

Psalm 27:1–4

Wow. David could have asked for anything. More weapons? More soldiers? Angels to watch over him? No. He said there was "one thing" above all else. And that was to seek the Lord, "to seek him in his temple."

God is our defender. We sing songs about this. He fights our battles, yes. I believe it! But how does it happen? It happens by our looking at the one thing. That one thing is Jesus.

This sounds too simple. If you and I will continue to make Jesus a priority in this very distracted day we are living in, we will hear His voice with clarity, and we will not be confused about what He is saying. I travel the world, and almost every week I am speaking in a different town or city. The number one question I get from the Body of Christ is, "What is God saying?" We wouldn't be so desperate to ask that question if we were focusing on the one thing—Jesus.

Prophetic Declaration and Prayer

I want to make this declaration with you, so join me in this prayer:

Father, I thank You for the person reading this right now. I thank You that You have created us to hear Your voice. We break every distraction off our lives and every attack off our minds!

Jesus, I declare that from this day forward, we will become more aware of You. In every situation of life, make us aware of Your voice, Your presence. I pray that in the midst of distractions and confusion, we would have a focus on You that cannot be breached.

One thing! One thing! Complete focus on You, Jesus!

Father, thank You that today marks a new level of focus and vision for us. We love You and thank You for this message. In Jesus' name. Amen.

Powerful Points about the Prophetic

- Since Steve Jobs announced the iPhone back in 2007, smartphones have become a weapon of mass distraction and mass destruction. Many people are today held prisoner to a small screen.
- The apostle Paul told us in 1 Corinthians 7:35 (NKJV) that we should "serve the Lord without distraction."
- I once heard the Lord say, *If you want to hear My voice, you must turn down the volume of the world!* Compared to His voice, how loud is the world to you and me?
- The lockdowns of 2020 forced people into isolation, and the Internet became their main source of entertainment. Their priorities changed as a result, and three areas of life suffered: *self-esteem, connection with people,* and *connection with God.*
- In the area of *self-esteem,* when you spend so much time online looking at everyone else's best moments, you can begin to feel bad about your own life.
- In the area of *connection with people,* the online world has become a fantasy world of sorts, causing people to lose real relationships because they aren't valuing or prioritizing those connections.
- The area of *connection with God* has seen by far the greatest attack of the enemy in recent times. Jesus gave us an essential key to receiving from God: *seeking Him first.* As we prioritize heaven, we will hear God's voice clearly and honor that voice.
- God isn't only interested in our outward expression to the Body of Christ. He wants just *you and me.* We can get so busy around Jesus that we fail just to *be.*
- "Be still, and know that I am God; I will be exalted among the nations, I will be exalted in the earth," God says in

Psalm 46:10. Sometimes we need just to *be* at Jesus' feet, as Mary chose to be, while her sister, Martha, was distracted by other things.

- You and I will accomplish more at Jesus' feet than anywhere else.

- The disciples were distracted by finding a meal while Jesus ministered to the woman at the well, who went on to impact her whole world (and ours). If we don't set the right priority, our own desires will pull us away from Jesus. A distracted life can cause us to miss the harvest.

- We have many responsibilities, but spiritually, we have only one. Like King David, we need to focus on one thing: seeking the Lord.

- If you and I will continue to make Jesus a priority in this very distracted day we are living in, we will hear His voice with clarity, and we will not be confused about what He is saying.

4

SEEING THROUGH THE STORM

The Value of Perseverance

A few years ago, I watched an interview with a world-renowned worship leader from Australia. She was sharing her testimony of overcoming cancer. It was a powerful testimony. She was through it all by then and was reflecting and testifying of all that the Lord had done for her. She was healed and had no remaining trace of cancer. It was an amazing story, and I was thanking God audibly as I was watching it. Then she said something I didn't quite understand: "In some ways, I miss those days of being sick and going through it [the cancer battle]. God was so near, and I heard His voice so clear."

What? That was a bit much for me to handle. How could a trial bring us closer to God? Why would God need to use that? I had so many questions at that time. Then I lived a few more years of life. And just as in the previous chapter, where we talked about the value of priority, in this chapter we will take another step toward hearing His voice clearly, this time by looking at the value of perseverance. We will show how perseverance and endurance are essential keys that will enable us to honor God and hear Him.

This "new creation" life we live means that we are conquerors. Romans 8:37 reminds us that "in all these things we are more than conquerors through him who loved us." That's right. You are more than a conqueror in Christ!

I have seen so many families over the years go through various trials and attacks, and I'll tell you, what you believe will determine where you go on the other side of life's difficulties. How you spend your time, the things you read, what you watch—all of these will play a role in determining how your trial ends. God designed you and me to endure and persevere through trials. That means when we are going through difficult times (which we all will), we can grow in faith with God, hear His voice through them and come out stronger on the other side. When we approach every storm as a conqueror, we will overcome.

Difficulties are hard for us. Especially this younger generation. Many young people are triggered by trials and often misinterpret them as a sign that they are not doing well. I have observed many younger people go through struggles when I knew they were on the right path. I knew that right around the corner was a breakthrough, and I would watch them—only to see them get discouraged, and in some cases even walk away from their faith. Right before a breakthrough!

"The grace has lifted," I would hear from them. Or, "I sense a new season is coming." Or, "Maybe I wasn't called to do that." These are all excuses people use to walk away from situations where God has called them to endure and to see breakthrough.

Things may appear difficult, but we have been given the power to overcome every situation. As we endure through the difficulties of life—the way God designed us to—we will hear His voice more clearly.

• Endurance versus Perseverance

We are called to do both. To endure and to persevere.

Enduring is experiencing or surviving something difficult. Persevering is continuing through it, even when you don't see the breakthrough you are believing for. In 2 Timothy 4:5, we find the apostle Paul writes, "But you, keep your head in all situations, endure hardship, do the work of an evangelist, discharge all the duties of your ministry."

Keep your head in all situations. Go through everything the Father has allowed and set before you. We are overcomers because Jesus has overcome the world. We now step into our place and walk in the power and authority He gave us, so we can go through every storm that may come.

The Bible says that as we are facing difficulties, it may appear tough, but actually it is not:

> But we have this treasure in jars of clay to show that this all-surpassing power is from God and not from us. We are hard pressed on every side, but not crushed; perplexed, but not in despair; persecuted, but not abandoned; struck down, but not destroyed. We always carry around in our body the death of Jesus, so that the life of Jesus may also be revealed in our body.
>
> 2 Corinthians 4:7–10

It may seem as if others are about to destroy you, but you will not be destroyed. That's what the Bible says. That means you may go through situations where it seems bad, but it isn't.

It may seem as if it's not going to work out, but it will. We will never be without challenges. We need to realize it's how we are designed to live—walking in power and overcoming in life.

Trials and difficulties are going to come in this world. They will not hurt us if we believe we have been given the power to overcome. I have seen many people increase their faith through challenges and draw nearer to God, which resulted in clarity in hearing His voice. In fact, I see two main things happen when we go through trials: our perspective changes, and we receive revelation. Let's look at these two things more closely.

1. Our perspective changes

Years ago, one of my leaders called the church and requested an emergency meeting. She was going through a lot and needed wisdom. Right before I left the office, she came to see me. As she sat down, she explained that life was difficult. She shared about employment challenges, challenges with an older child, and financial issues. This leader was feeling very, very overwhelmed.

She told me she was being "attacked," and wondered if it might even be happening because of a curse on her. After about thirty minutes of sharing all she was facing, she asked me, "What do you think about all of this?"

"Well," I said, "I don't think this is really an attack from the devil."

"Really?" she replied. "Then what is it?" she asked, eagerly wanting to know.

"It's just life," I answered. "This is regular life that you have allowed to become so challenging in your mind."

In no way was I downplaying her feelings. I realized that although this storm was so real to her, she needed to realize the perspective of heaven—the way God has designed us to overcome. Although what we go through may seem like intense pressure at the time, ultimately, we are going to overcome every situation. Because God designed us to overcome. As we endure and push through it, we will be closer to Him and see His hand move in greater ways in us. We will hear Him more clearly. We have to embrace every season and realize that it's only temporary. Don't allow your trials to taint your perspective.

When winter comes, the leaves have fallen and the trees are left empty and gray. Some view this as an ugly change. Let me tell you, it is not. One of my friends bought a house in Colorado. It was stunning and beautiful in the summer, but as the winter season approached, he told me he had started feeling a bit discouraged about the long winter ahead.

A few days later, he called to say that all the leaves had fallen off the trees in his backyard, and as a result, he now could see mountains! He had no clue that the mountains could be viewed from his house. He regretted complaining a few days earlier, and later would say, "The winter season has a way of showing us an amazing perspective that we wouldn't have seen otherwise."

There is a perspective in the midst of your storm that God wants you to see. He has designed you to see and to hear, and to overcome.

2. We receive revelation

In no way am I telling you that we need to struggle to get anything from God. I am telling you that as we go through various trials and storms, God is with you and has equipped you to overcome!

I remember years ago when we purchased our building in New London, Connecticut. It was an older building, over two hundred years old. I remember removing all the pews, and unfortunately, removing all the hymnals also. At the time I didn't want any trace of old religion. Then one day, someone came into my office and told me that as the volunteers were cleaning, they discovered one of the old hymnals. This person asked me if I wanted it thrown out. Regretting my original decision, I instructed him to give it to me.

As he left the office, I looked at this old hymnal. Not familiar with many hymns, I wondered what would happen if I just opened the book randomly and read some of the songs like a tweet. I spent the next hour in a puddle of tears. I was blown away by the powerful lyrics! I could feel the power through these writers to overcome. Many words on the blood of Jesus, and the cross—it was amazing. I could feel the power these psalmists felt when they were writing the hymns.

Today, many worship leaders and songwriters have tapped into feelings over the Word. It's easy to write a song about your personal feelings, almost narcissistic in nature. These hymns I was reading were not about the individual writers or about us; they were about God, Jesus, the Holy Spirit, the blood, the Word and the cross. They reminded me of Isaiah 61:3:

> . . . and provide for those who grieve in Zion—to bestow on them a crown of beauty instead of ashes, the oil of joy instead of mourning, and a garment of praise instead of a spirit of despair. They will be called oaks of righteousness, a planting of the LORD for the display of his splendor.

It is time to exchange our garments of despair for praise.

Perseverance through Pentecost

I am so thankful for the Day of Pentecost. Jesus said to His disciples (and all of us who would follow), "But you will receive power when the Holy Spirit comes on you; and you will be my witnesses in Jerusalem, and in all Judea and Samaria, and to the ends of the earth" (Acts 1:8).

All the disciples knew was that there would be power for witnessing. They didn't even know that tongues of fire were about to fall. Yet the early Church embraced power for the next season. It can be easy for us to walk away from reading about the Day of Pentecost and think it was only about a language (tongues). However, it was about the power that Jesus said we would have.

The Day of Pentecost was ultimately the day from which the Holy Spirit would come to dwell within us forever. It was a mutual indwelling, a filling that would not end. From that moment on, we would have Jesus dwelling inside us. This would be for witnessing, but it would also be for perseverance and endurance, so we could overcome every situation we face. This means that again, whatever you will go through, God has filled you to overcome.

We saw the early Church go through persecution, with many believers dying for their faith. This only produced greater faith and allowed the Gospel to go farther. In one aspect, the Gospel expanded greatly. Here's one recorded instance: "This went on for two years, so that all the Jews and Greeks who lived in the province of Asia heard the word of the Lord" (Acts 19:10).

That's amazing. One of the benefits from Acts 2 was power to witness. Imagine how focused you have to be for it to be said about you that because of your perseverance, everyone in your geographic area heard the Gospel! That's incredible. However, Acts 14:22 also tells us, "We must go through many hardships to enter the kingdom of God."

Wow. The same group who went out and saw regions shaken and saw many miracles also went through tremendous difficulty. As we know, God was with them. Acts 2 also gave the early Church (and us) power to endure. If we look at difficulty as an obstacle, we will never be able to move mountains. If we endure, however, we will continue as overcomers and hear God's voice through it all.

Discernment is vital for the day we are living in. Discernment about what God is doing or saying is essential. I can tell where many Christians are by what they are saying, responding to and reacting to. We have already learned that what we behold, we become. What we focus on will dominate us, good or bad. This is why we need discernment to endure. We are walking as overcomers, not just going through life and trying to get through a season.

One day I confronted a member of our church whom we hadn't seen in a while. I genuinely cared for him, and I also knew he had a great destiny in God. "How are you?" I asked.

"Okay," he replied. "I'm just in a holding pattern, you know, a season changing."

Friend, can I tell you there is no such thing as a holding pattern? Some people have been in a "season" or "shift" for forty years! It is time to break out and overcome. It is time to discern properly and advance the Kingdom. We see an amazing story in the book of Matthew about discernment:

Immediately Jesus made the disciples get into the boat and go on ahead of him to the other side, while he dismissed the crowd. After he had dismissed them, he went up on a mountainside by himself to pray. Later that night, he was there alone, and the boat was already a considerable distance from land, buffeted by the waves because the wind was against it.

Shortly before dawn Jesus went out to them, walking on the lake. When the disciples saw him walking on the lake, they were terrified. "It's a ghost," they said, and cried out in fear.

But Jesus immediately said to them: "Take courage! It is I. Don't be afraid."

"Lord, if it's you," Peter replied, "tell me to come to you on the water."

"Come," he said.

Then Peter got down out of the boat, walked on the water and came toward Jesus. But when he saw the wind, he was afraid and, beginning to sink, cried out, "Lord, save me!"

Immediately Jesus reached out his hand and caught him. "You of little faith," he said, "why did you doubt?"

And when they climbed into the boat, the wind died down. Then those who were in the boat worshiped him, saying, "Truly you are the Son of God."

When they had crossed over, they landed at Gennesaret. And when the men of that place recognized Jesus, they sent word to all the surrounding country. People brought all their sick to him and begged him to let the sick just touch the edge of his cloak, and all who touched it were healed.

Matthew 14:22–36

This is such a powerful story. First of all, Jesus told the disciples to get into the boat and go to the other side. There should have been no confusion about what their assignment was. Jesus was telling them what they were going to do. He spoke His word. He told them to go ahead of Him (implying that He would be coming later). You'd think that would be enough. Nope. Just a few moments later, the wind and waves start beating on the boat, and just before dawn, Jesus walks over to them on the water.

The disciples called Him a "ghost." They really did, despite Jesus' telling them earlier what would be happening! When we go through trials and storms, it gets hard to discern, as we just saw with the disciples. It didn't matter what they had seen or heard earlier; they were not discerning properly amid the wind and waves.

Jesus then said, "Don't be afraid." He was speaking His word to calm the storm within them. He was longing for them to see clearly. They were scared; they were afraid. Jesus not only told them they were getting in the boat; He also commanded that they not be afraid.

Peter then asked Jesus to tell him to come. When he heard the Lord say "Come," he began to walk on the water.

Peter wasn't walking on the water, however. He was walking on the *Word*.

This is exactly what I am believing for through this chapter, that you would—amid the winds and waves—hear God's voice and see miracles. If we aren't looking and listening, we will be misled by our feelings. Jesus isn't a ghost. He never was or will be. However, fear will cause us to lack discernment. When we realize that God's desire is to speak to us in any storm, we will be quicker to endure and persevere with Him. Matthew 24:13 says, "But the one who stands firm to the end will be saved."

Stand on Your Story!

One night shortly after giving my life to Jesus, I was at church. We were worshiping, and I felt God's presence so strongly. I began to weep, overcome with His love. I remember having a deep longing to be used by God. It was so strong.

A week earlier, I had received my first prophetic word. My pastor walked up to me at church and said, "God is going to give you a voice, to speak His Word."

I was so moved with joy and gratitude. Here I was, a young kid from the projects who had just gotten saved, hearing that

God would somehow use me to do something for Him. That word set the stage for my life with God.

A few weeks later, I was at a youth event with our church, and a guest minister was speaking. Honestly, I don't remember what he said, but I remember he gave an altar call, and I went up to the front. A few moments later, as he was praying for people in the crowd, he walked up to me. He went back to grab the microphone and began to give me a prophetic word publicly. "There is a call of God on your life, and the Lord is telling me that He has given you a voice, a voice to speak His Word!"

I was very moved, and clearly this was a confirmation of the word I had gotten earlier in the week. However, he continued further: "You will go through many trials and storms . . . many. You will face betrayal and loss, and I see all of these trials and storms becoming a platform that you will speak from." He continued, "Endure, persevere, and the Lord will use everything you will face as a message of hope and deliverance to a lost and hurting generation."

As a teenager, I wasn't sure how to take all of this. As an older man now, I am certain that God was speaking, and I can see how He has used, and continues to use, all that we face in life for His glory. It's not about us, but what He can do through our lives if we submit to Him.

He is the potter; we are the clay. This life is amazing and unpredictable. All we have is our yes. And I can without a doubt tell you that going through these storms of life has opened up the Lord's voice in my life and has brought clarity to that voice.

Get ready! Get ready to hear God clearly, even in the midst of every storm of life. Get ready to stand on your story! Get ready to come through every situation with a greater anointing and authority! Endure and persevere!

Prophetic Declaration and Prayer

Father, I thank You today for Your power and authority in our lives. I thank You that every storm we are facing today You have already empowered us to overcome. I declare today that fear is broken, and shame is broken, and we will receive Your love today in a new way. We will see the goodness of the Lord in the land of the living. We will step into a new realm of Your presence and hear Your voice clearly.

I thank You that everything we have faced, everything we are facing, and everything we will face, will be a memorial before You. Our story will be a platform where many people will be touched and changed! We thank You for this, in Jesus' mighty name. Amen.

Powerful Points about the Prophetic

- We need to value perseverance. Perseverance and endurance are essential keys that will enable us to honor God and hear His voice.

- When we are going through difficult times (which we all will), we can grow in faith with God, hear His voice through them and come out stronger on the other side.

- Things may appear difficult, but we have been given the power to overcome every situation. As we endure through the difficulties of life—the way God designed us to—we will hear His voice more clearly.

- Enduring is experiencing or surviving something difficult. Persevering is continuing through it, even when you don't see the breakthrough you are believing for. We are called to do both. To endure and to persevere.

- Trials and difficulties are going to come in this world. They will not hurt us if we believe we have been given the power to overcome.

- Two main things happen when we go through trials: our perspective changes, and we receive revelation. There is a perspective through your storm that God wants you to see. And even though you don't need to struggle to get anything from God, you will hear His voice more clearly as you persevere.

- We have to embrace every season and realize that it's only temporary. Don't allow your trials to taint your perspective.

- The early Church embraced power for the next season on the Day of Pentecost. It can be easy for us to walk away from reading about that day and think it was about a language (tongues). However, it was about the power that Jesus said we would have.

- The Day of Pentecost is the day the Holy Spirit came to dwell inside us forever. This absolutely is for witnessing, but it is also for perseverance and endurance, so we can overcome every situation we face.
- If we look at difficulty as an obstacle, we will never be able to move mountains. If we endure, however, we will continue as overcomers and hear God's voice through it all.
- Discernment is vital for the day we are living in. Discernment about what God is doing or saying is essential. It is time to discern properly and advance the Kingdom.
- God is the potter; we are the clay. This life is amazing and unpredictable. All we have is our yes. And going through the storms of life will open up the Lord's voice in our life and bring clarity to that voice.
- Get ready to hear God clearly, even in the midst of every storm of life. Get ready to stand on your story! Get ready to come through every situation with a greater anointing and authority! Endure and persevere!

5

THE POWER
OF PEACE

The Value of Emotional Health

Peace. What happened to it? Where did it go?

In the past few years, as a pastor, I have been heartbroken to see people all over the world lose their minds and their peace. Torment, poor emotional health, bipolar disorder, depression, anxiety, PTSD, mental health issues—all appear to be valid. Trauma is real, and chemical changes in your brain and body are real, but they are not a greater reality than the blood of Jesus.

Take a look at these startling statistics that show just how widespread emotional issues and a lack of peace are in America.[1] And I believe the stats in many other countries around the world would show something similar.

- 15 percent of people in the United States are on an antidepressant medication.

- Over 50 percent of millennials are in consistent therapy [with a worldly therapist].
- Marijuana is the most commonly used federally illegal drug in the U.S., with about 50 million users.
- 20 percent of Americans claim to have used marijuana at least once since 2019.
- A staggering 85 percent of adults claim to have drunk alcohol in their life.
- 50 percent of adults 18–22 have consumed alcohol in the last month.
- Suicide attempts among adolescents surged by more than 50 percent in 2020.

In some cases, these numbers are higher in the Church. I have helped people from all aspects of life who have been involved in deep trauma, abuse, rape, abandonment, even murder. I will tell you that you cannot get free outside the power of Jesus!

In no way am I telling you that medications won't help, or that therapy doesn't have any place. I am telling you that they don't help if they are your only plan. What happens is that we get caught up in a pattern of medication and addressing the symptoms and the manifestations, so we never get into the place of true peace. God desires to heal our minds through His mighty power, bringing us His peace. Our emotional health matters to Him.

Without debating about what level of torment we may or may not be experiencing, what we need to do is agree that Jesus wants us to be emotionally strong. He wants us to be clear in our minds and at peace. So how we view our emotional health matters. God is good and the devil is bad, and torment comes from the pit of hell. We cannot develop a tolerance for any type of mental or emotional torment.

We are called to cast out devils, not counsel them. Deliverance is needed today more than ever, yet there is a whole generation only wanting to deal with the symptoms (feelings) and not with the root. I believe with all the current shaking we are seeing among well-known people of God and movements in the Body of Christ, it is essential that we hold fast to our discernment about what spirit and power is influencing us.

There is a place for deliverance today, just as there was in Jesus' day. Let me say, however, that clearly, not every person struggling with mental health issues has a demon. Yet we don't believe God is the source of any such attacks or medical conditions. If we believe that God is not the source and that He can heal and deliver, then we will be better equipped to handle any and all manifestations of illness or torment that arise around our minds.

In the same way, we cannot tolerate the influence of alcohol and drugs on our minds and emotions. Any tolerance will further open us up to the enemy's attacks. In the end, it is important to know that God is our life source and desires to heal us.

Having God's peace is essential to walking in victory, and especially to hearing the voice of the Lord. Peace allows our hearts to be still and calm so that His voice can become clearer to us.

Peace Is a Gift

The first thing we must realize about peace is that it is a gift. It is a free gift that Jesus paid for on the cross. It is also a fruit of the Spirit. Galatians 5:22–23 reads, "But the fruit of the Spirit is love, joy, peace, forbearance, kindness, goodness, faithfulness, gentleness and self-control. Against such things there is no law."

We see that peace is classified as a gift and a fruit of the Spirit. Jesus also opened our eyes even further about peace when He spoke this about it: "I leave the gift of peace with you—my peace. Not the kind of fragile peace given by the world, but my perfect peace. Don't yield to fear or be troubled in your hearts—instead, be courageous!" (John 14:27 TPT).

That's it! Peace is a gift that only Jesus can give. Comfort is similar:

> Blessed be the God and Father of our Lord Jesus Christ, the Father of mercies and God of all comfort, who comforts us in all our tribulation, that we may be able to comfort those who are in any trouble, with the comfort with which we ourselves are comforted by God. For as the sufferings of Christ abound in us, so our consolation also abounds through Christ.
>
> 2 Corinthians 1:3–5 NKJV

When this passage says "God of all comfort," it means there is no other author or source of such comfort available to anyone. All true comfort originates with Him. Peace is the same. He is the God of all peace. When we realize that peace is a gift from God, we can ensure that through every situation of life, we maintain and keep our peace.

Prophetic or Possessed?

Years ago, we had a boy in the church who was diagnosed with mental issues. He was on and off medication, and his emotional health was suffering. For most of his life he had been labeled by doctors, and what had started with a different label had turned "suicidal." One day, I received a call from his mom that this young man was in a mental health ward in the hospital, on suicide watch. The mom wanted me to go pray for her son. As I was driving over to the hospital, the Lord said, *Tell him he is not crazy or bipolar. Tell him he is designed by Me, to hear My voice.*

It hit me as I began to realize that all the labels the doctors had put on this boy had become demonic prophetic words that the family believed. I walked in, and he looked at me with despair. His hands were tied up so he wouldn't hurt himself. I could see the tears running down his face, and I knew this wasn't who he was.

I looked right at him and said, "You are not crazy! Do you hear me?" I said it again, but louder, "*You are not crazy!* You have been designed by God to hear His voice, and I break off every curse and lie that has been spoken over you!"

Immediately, he snapped. It was as if his eyes were no longer glossy, and he was completely in his right mind. He was healed.

I walked away realizing that we have to expose the demonic attack that can lie at the root of mental illness. It is a demon that torments people's minds. Let me say again that there can be a place for medication and therapy, which can help manage the symptoms. But again, those things can't be the only plan, because they don't deal with the root issue. For that, you need the blood of Jesus and its healing power. Understanding the root doesn't mean we don't love and sympathize with those who battle illness, but we cannot let up from believing for a miracle.

One of my good friends was conceived in a mental institution. Yes, you read that right. His mom and dad were both patients in a mental institution and were not supposed to be together at all! And they got pregnant. It was said that the child would never be in his right mind. Well, let me tell you, he is a youth pastor today.

And I remember the day we were at a prayer meeting at our house, and his mom came up to me. She would come to church and sit in the farthest seat from the front. She sat there lifeless; you could see it in her eyes. That night she came, and we asked at the end of the meeting if we could pray for her. I will never forget when God set her free. In an instant, she snapped out of it, and she began talking and communicating clearly.

Our emotional health is so important to Jesus. Today, we are being driven as a society to accommodate illness over healing. I believe many people suffer beyond their level of control, on very severe levels. Although we want to love and pray for everyone in that condition, sometimes there can still be a demon at work, which will require the application of a spiritual remedy beyond any medical remedy—the power and healing in the blood of Jesus.

What We Watch, and What We Hear

We often don't realize how important our emotional health is to God, or how important our peace is. We also don't realize how important it is for us to do all we can to maintain our emotional health and peace. I believe that even what we watch and what we hear can either add to our emotional health and peace or take away from them.

Have you ever watched a movie or listened to a song and immediately felt sick or felt a sense of evil, as if something wasn't right? Many times, this is the Holy Spirit warning us that we have to shut off whatever it is and focus on Jesus instead. Evil spirits can attack us through what we watch or hear. I'm not saying a demon will possess you because of it; it won't. But your emotional health and peace will certainly come under attack. And losing those can impair your relationships, your ministry and your decision making.

Isaiah 26:3 says, "You will keep in perfect peace those whose minds are steadfast, because they trust in you." Having such perfect peace is the Father's desire for our emotional health. What starts as a stressful situation in our lives, or even as something we expose ourselves to through entertainment or another avenue, can take root in our heart and mind, and then we find ourselves without peace. Keeping our mind steadfast on God is the secret to unlocking our emotional health.

"Idle minds are the devil's playground," I used to hear in church. As believers, we should guard not just our heart, but our mind. In the lockdowns of 2020, so many people found themselves with extra time on their hands. Unfortunately, that often became extra time for the devil also, as many people filled that time with things they otherwise might not have been watching or listening to. When we find ourselves stressed and filled with drama instead of peace, it's a sign our emotional health is suffering. And it's a reminder that we need to keep our mind on God rather than on things that can make us emotionally unhealthy.

We need to realize the power of our mind. One of my favorite Scriptures is Romans 10:17, which I quoted in chapter 1. Let's look at it again: "So then faith comes by hearing, and hearing by the word of God" (NKJV). What we hear is so vital to our faith and mind. If faith comes through hearing, so does fear. And fear will attack our mind and steal our peace.

What we focus on matters. What we allow into our lives will ultimately affect our emotional state. What are you watching? What are you listening to? With all of the issues in today's culture, I feel we must guard our mind just as much as we guard our heart. Our mind needs to be transformed and healthy so we can accomplish all God has for us to do on this earth.

Everyone Faces Emotional Pain

We all face emotional pain of some sort. Everyone's family experiences pain and hurt. I faced it early on in my family. My mother was born deaf. She also had scleroderma and osteoporosis, and at a young age her hands and feet were crippled with rheumatoid arthritis. So I grew up with a severely handicapped mother.

Then my son Luke was born profoundly deaf. I can't explain the pain of growing up with a deaf mom and now having my son face the same challenge. That was emotionally traumatic for me, but what I didn't do was respond by letting it steal my faith or peace. I also didn't give my life to bring awareness to deaf culture, although with my mom and Luke both being deaf, I am very familiar with what that culture is like and all it involves. I love deaf people. I have a soft place in my heart for them. To this day, if I see someone deaf struggling to communicate out in society, I will step in and help sign and talk for them. I learned American Sign Language (ASL) before I could speak English.

Even with all that emotional pain, however, I found peace in trusting God. I found a place where I could love my family members as if they never had a disability, while standing in the gap for a miracle. My son now has cochlear implants and can speak and communicate clearly. Thank God for the miracle of implants! Even with that, we are constantly praying and believing for a miracle. We have seen many deaf ears healed, and I have a promise that we will see that with our son.

I want to mention here that sometimes the emotional health of pastors and ministers is at great risk. When we see accusations come against them, and even when we see some of the well-known ones come out and admit to adultery, money laundering and other crimes, we must realize that they are human beings, not just public names. I have known ministers who started out strong and full of faith, only to find themselves stressed emotionally and then attacked in their minds. (And I know firsthand how traumatizing this can be.) Many of them don't even recognize the attacks of the devil on their emotional health.

What we need to do is pray for pastors and ministers. Lift them up daily before the Lord. The emotional health of our spiritual leaders is so important to the Lord, and poor emotional health can absolutely hinder their ability to hear from God. There is never an excuse for sin, period! Yet these leaders are on the front lines of battle, and they need our prayers more than ever before.

Stepping into Peace

What aspects of your life do you need to take to a place of peace where you can hear God's voice?

You may not have a lot of sickness around you. Maybe it's poverty instead, or divorce, trauma, abuse, rape or even a horrific death or crime. Through every season in life, there is a safe place in God's presence that will cultivate hearing His voice. Psalm 91:1–11 (NKJV) gives us a beautiful promise:

> He who dwells in the secret place of the Most High shall abide under the shadow of the Almighty. I will say of the

L<small>ORD</small>, "He is my refuge and my fortress; my God, in Him I will trust."

Surely He shall deliver you from the snare of the fowler and from the perilous pestilence. He shall cover you with His feathers, and under His wings you shall take refuge; His truth shall be your shield and buckler. You shall not be afraid of the terror by night, nor of the arrow that flies by day, nor of the pestilence that walks in darkness, nor of the destruction that lays waste at noonday.

A thousand may fall at your side, and ten thousand at your right hand; but it shall not come near you. Only with your eyes shall you look, and see the reward of the wicked.

Because you have made the L<small>ORD</small>, who is my refuge, even the Most High, your dwelling place, no evil shall befall you, nor shall any plague come near your dwelling; for He shall give His angels charge over you, to keep you in all your ways.

In this psalm we find so many promises of protection, covering and discernment. They're all found through one position—abiding! Anxious thoughts, fear, attacks, trials will all steal our peace and hinder the voice of God in our lives. Abiding under His wings, staying under His covering of peace, keeps us clean and able to hear His voice.

Truthfully, since 2020 we have been forced either to walk in peace and hear God's voice or to live in fear. It's one or the other. So step into peace! In chapter 3 we already talked about setting priorities, and this will continue to be a theme for us moving forward in peace.

Our Thought Life

Peace has everything to do with our thoughts. What we allow to enter our mind in a single day matters. The book of Romans reminds us that it is with our mind we serve the Lord (see Romans 7:25). More people are struggling in the area of their thoughts than any other area. It is the mental-health battle. We heavily focus on the major mental illnesses, but depression and anxiety are the killers in our culture.

We were never meant to see so many images in a single day. You can scroll on your phone and see a cute cat playing outside, and then see someone getting horribly beaten up, all within a few seconds. The instant availability of all these images has produced a gateway for the devil to come in and torment a generation. Thoughts can change our lives.

Think about your imagination. It is a powerful tool. On the one hand, we can use our imagination for evil—every murder starts with a thought. Marriages are destroyed, lives are ruined because of a thought. On the other hand, thoughts can also transform our lives, regions and nations! I remember back in 2017, I was working out on the treadmill one day and had a thought. As I was listening to one of my favorite sports podcasts, something about hearing the powerful voice in a headphone moved me. Then a thought came: *What if I did a podcast? Every day? What if I shared a brief thought every day to encourage people and allow them to draw closer to God?*

From that thought, I decided to record our first episode of *Engaging Heaven Today*. Millions of downloads later, with multiple devotions put into print as a result, those early thoughts have changed the lives of thousands. (If you want to find my current podcast, it is now called *Engage Heaven*.) Thoughts can open the door or close the door to the Lord.

Thoughts on Jesus

Luke tells us an amazing story about Jesus that demonstrates the power of our thoughts:

So He came to Nazareth, where He had been brought up. And as His custom was, He went into the synagogue on the Sabbath day, and stood up to read. And He was handed the book of the prophet Isaiah. And when He had opened the book, He found the place where it was written:

> "The Spirit of the LORD is upon Me,
> Because He has anointed Me
> To preach the gospel to the poor;
> He has sent Me to heal the brokenhearted,
> To proclaim liberty to the captives
> And recovery of sight to the blind,
> To set at liberty those who are oppressed;
> To proclaim the acceptable year of the LORD."

Then He closed the book, and gave it back to the attendant and sat down. And the eyes of all who were in the synagogue were fixed on Him. And He began to say to them, "Today this Scripture is fulfilled in your hearing." So all bore witness to Him, and marveled at the gracious words which proceeded out of His mouth. And they said, "Is this not Joseph's son?

Luke 4:16–22 NKJV

Can you imagine being in that room and seeing Jesus read a scroll? Although it was customary for someone to do so, there was something about His voice that was different from all others. In fact, the Bible says the people "marveled" at His voice (see Luke 4:32; Matthew 8:27). Israel was in darkness, and the people hearing Him were not sure if He was the Messiah or not. But for a moment, they felt it.

Can you imagine having the thought and feeling that could break a nation out of silence? They had it that day. The issue was not their healthy thought about how marvelous He was, however. It was how quickly their unhealthy thought followed! The one where they said, "Is this not Joseph's son?" (verse 22). That's all it took. They went from Jesus possibly being the Messiah to Jesus being just an average son, in all but seconds. In the same way, our thought life can either bring in the floodgates of heaven—or hell. Usually, there's not much space in between those conflicting thought patterns.

The battle, although very much natural for us, is not actually natural. It is a spiritual battle, and we have to wage a spiritual war. Romans 12:2 reminds us that we are transformed by our mind being renewed. We have to live in a place of constantly renewing our mind. We are also reminded in 2 Corinthians 10:4–5 (NKJV),

> For the weapons of our warfare are not carnal but mighty in God for pulling down strongholds, casting down arguments and every high thing that exalts itself against the knowledge of God, bringing every thought into captivity to the obedience of Christ.

We are called to cast down every imagined thing that exalts itself above the Lord. It is impossible to hear the voice of God clearly when we have other voices competing and our imagination exalting itself above the Lord. If our imagination and thoughts are not guarded and sanctified, we cannot discern properly.

Hearing from the Place of His Presence

Years ago, before I ever learned to hear the voice of God, I always struggled to understand what He was saying. Then one day I was in a service where at the end of the meeting, the minister told everyone we were about to "see" in the Spirit.

He instructed everyone just to worship—silently. Actually, he told us not to shake, move or pray aloud. He wanted everyone to be still in God's presence.

When the room was quiet, this minister said, "Come, Holy Spirit," and at that moment, for the first time, images and pictures from heaven flooded my mind. I realized there was a direct connection between being still in our thoughts and minds, and hearing God. Then I remembered the story of Samuel. In 1 Samuel 3:1–5 (NKJV), we see a picture of Eli the priest hiding the sins of his sons. God should have been speaking to him, but Eli wasn't listening and was disobedient. The Bible says,

> Now the boy Samuel ministered to the LORD before Eli. And the word of the LORD was rare in those days; there was no widespread revelation. And it came to pass at that time, while Eli was lying down in his place, and when his eyes had begun to grow so dim that he could not see, and before the lamp of God went out in the tabernacle of the LORD where the ark of God was, and while Samuel was lying down, that the LORD called Samuel. And he answered, "Here I am!" So he ran to Eli and said, "Here I am, for you called me."

This is a picture of two very different postures. The Bible says one person, Eli, is lying down "in his place," which in his case was prophetic of a place without peace. When we are in this posture, in our own place, sin abounds and we are blind spiritually to what the Lord is doing. (Eli was, in fact, also blind physically.) This can happen in any place of life.

Then there is Samuel. Samuel is lying down also, except he is lying down near the tabernacle, in the place of God's presence. Prophetically, it was a place full of peace, and this had everything to do with hearing God. When we are doing what God has called us to do, and being obedient, we are in a place of peace. Samuel was postured to hear, and as a result, the Lord spoke to him and broke many years of silence.

Are you positioned to hear? Do you have peace? As a pastor, I see so many people "lying down" in regret. I see people "lying down" in sin and trauma. There is no peace, and as a result, they are not able to hear the voice of God.

Where Did You Leave Your Peace?

During a Tuesday night service at one of our locations, a woman came up and shared a vision about what she saw. She saw a beach with nice white sand, and on this beach were a pair of sandals. In front of the sandals were footprints. And they were seen going far ahead of the sandals. It looked as if someone had walked away and left his or her sandals behind. The Lord spoke to her and said, *Tell the people the sandals represent My peace, and I need them to go back and get their peace.*

It was a powerful vision. Because of it, many people realized that they had walked away from the place of God's peace. Many were able to "go back" and realize what had happened that caused them to lose peace. Many were empowered to receive the peace that had been available all along. And as a result, they were able to begin to speak peace in every situation.

In the book of Mark, we see Jesus, who was sleeping in a boat, wake up to a disturbance. The disciples were scared and concerned about a storm. "Then He arose and rebuked the wind, and said to the sea, 'Peace, be still!' And the wind ceased and there was a great calm" (Mark 4:39 NKJV).

Jesus was showing us that what was inside Him—peace—began to transform what was around Him. That's how peace works. It starts on the inside, and then manifests through the hearing of His voice, followed by miracles. The bottom line is, we need peace to continue to hear God's voice. Our emotional health matters. And I believe God will heal any attacks on your mind, and you will hear God more clearly than ever before.

Prophetic Declaration and Prayer

Father, we thank You that You have created us and designed us to hear Your voice. We break every attack off our minds, and we declare that we will have no other mind than the mind of Christ!

We receive the peace that Jesus paid for on the cross, and we thank You from this moment forward that we will never step away from peace and the emotional health it brings. Through every storm of life, we will be victorious! In Jesus' mighty name! Amen.

Powerful Points about the Prophetic

- Trauma is real, and chemical changes in your brain and body are real, but they are not a greater reality than the blood of Jesus.

- Peace is essential to walking in victory, and especially to hearing the voice of the Lord. Peace allows our hearts to be still and calm so His voice can become clearer to us.

- The first thing we must realize about peace is that it is a gift. It is a free gift that Jesus paid for on the cross. It is also a fruit of the Spirit.

- There is a place for medication and therapy, which can help manage symptoms. But those can't be the only plan for mental or emotional trauma, because they don't deal with the root issue. For that, you need the blood of Jesus and its healing power.

- Today, we are being driven as a society to accommodate illness over healing. We don't realize how important it is for us to do all we can to maintain our emotional and mental health.

- I believe that even what we watch and what we hear can either add to our emotional health and peace or take away from them.

- Isaiah 26:3 says, "You will keep in perfect peace those whose minds are steadfast, because they trust in you." Keeping our mind steadfast on God is the secret to unlocking our emotional health.

- What we allow into our lives will ultimately affect our emotional state. What are you watching? What are you listening to? We must guard our mind just as much as we guard our heart.

- As Psalm 91 beautifully promises us, through every season in life there is a safe place in God's presence that will cultivate our hearing His voice.

- Anxious thoughts, fear, attacks, trials will all steal our peace and hinder the voice of God in our lives. Abiding under His wings, staying under His covering of peace, keeps us clean and able to hear His voice.

- Our thought life can either bring in the floodgates of heaven—or hell. Usually, there's not much space in between those conflicting thought patterns.

- It is impossible to hear the voice of God clearly when we have other voices competing and our imagination exalting itself above the Lord. If our imagination and thoughts are not guarded and sanctified, we cannot discern properly.

- Peace starts on the inside, and then manifests through the hearing of God's voice, followed by miracles. The bottom line is, we need peace to continue to hear God's voice.

- Our emotional health matters to God, and we need to recognize its value. I believe God will heal any attacks on your mind and emotions, and you will hear Him more clearly than ever before.

6

CONNECTION

The Value of Relationship

Connection. Human Connection. We all need it, and whether you realize it or not, we all long for it. We were designed to connect. With God, and with others.

We have already discussed the extreme dangers of a distracted life. What about human relationships? How important is the power of personal touch? The great T. L. Osborne shared a story of how he would send evangelists into the villages on the mission field, with what was essentially a tape recorder. When they pressed Play, it would begin a Gospel message Osborne would be speaking in the language of that nation. He spoke many dialects. What the evangelists realized, however, was more astounding. They realized that although the tape recorder was good, it wasn't as powerful as a person speaking the Gospel in person. Everyone wanted to talk to someone and not just listen to a tape recorder. Osborne called this "the power of personal touch."

Today, I believe many people struggle in the area of connection. As a pastor, I realize the largest church is the unchurched. There has been a disgruntled movement against the gift of church. People have been hurt, and in many circumstances, online church has replaced attending in person. But at what cost?

We talked in chapter 3 about Proverbs 18:1 (NKJV), which again says, "A man who isolates himself seeks his own desire; he rages against all wise judgment." As we saw in this Scripture, isolation in any form will "destroy" your sound judgment. Many people today have a lack of discernment that is directly connected to isolation. When you are alone (willingly or unwillingly), you begin to seek your own desires and not the Kingdom's. We have to connect with one another so we can have better clarity and discernment.

Proverbs 11:14 (NKJV) says, "Where there is no counsel, the people fall; but in the multitude of counselors there is safety." *No counsel* means being alone, isolated. Dare I say *quarantined . . . ?*

I know this sounds apocalyptic and straight end times, but what if I had told you before it happened that for Easter 2020, most of the churches in the world would be shut down? Who would ever have believed that until it actually happened? Yet in 2020, because of a virus, we saw many churches close their doors, and truthfully, to this day they have never recovered. People across the world were on lockdown. This was demonic politically, and the effects on people were astounding.

As a pastor, I could see the difference between people who stayed in personal fellowship versus people who were scared, hiding at home or simply trying to obey a government order. I believe those of us who are pastors have a greater responsibility to create a place where people can connect with

God—and with one another. We were created for personal fellowship and wisdom.

• Spiritual Fathering and Mothering

By far, one of the greatest needs I see today is fathering for a generation. Many people both young and old suffer today from a lack of fathering . . . and mentoring. Shortly after I was born again, I had a vision. In this vision I saw a map of America, and then I saw mature oak trees spring up across the map. Big, solid, mature trees. Next, I began to see young trees sprouting up next to the mature trees. Some of the young trees grew some distance away from the mature ones, however, while others grew right next to the taller, more mature ones. Next, I began to see the smaller trees that were not connected to the tall trees begin to die. And then they disappeared.

The Lord showed me that the tall trees were spiritual fathers and mothers, and the young trees were a younger generation. God designed all of us to grow together. However, where the young trees grew alone and isolated, they would die. God was sharing with me the importance of having mentors in our lives. I was determined to find some mentors for myself. I knew God wanted me to grow healthy.

At the time, I was in an Assembly of God church, and I knew that I wouldn't be able to fit within the framework of what that denomination was asking me to do to become a minister. I was very young and we had kids, yet I burned for the streets and for seeing miracles. I knew I wouldn't be able to do what was needed to become a minister where I was, so I decided to write a letter to the superintendent of the Assemblies of God. I wrote a long letter to Dr. Thomas Trask, basically the head of the Assemblies at that time, and someone who had been in ministry for sixty years. I explained my situation and how, in the current state of the organization, there was no room for "street preachers," people like me who caught the fire of God and were ready to blaze trails out on the streets. I asked him for genuine advice on what to do.

Dr. Trask responded with a handwritten letter in which he acknowledged me and advised that I needed to believe God for a real spiritual father, as Paul had been to Timothy. Dr. Trask believed that God had anointed me, and he believed that I would be further equipped by this fathering relationship.

Paul the apostle said in 1 Corinthians 4:15 (NKJV), "For though you might have ten thousand instructors in Christ, yet you do not have many fathers; for in Christ Jesus I have begotten you through the gospel." This is exactly what Dr. Trask was saying to me in his letter. Instructors are needed, and honestly, they are everywhere. However, there are not many spiritual fathers. We have a fathering issue in Christianity.

Around that time, little did I know that there was a pastor in West Haven, Connecticut, who was prophesying about me. He was telling his large congregation that God was sending a "son" of the house who would help usher in revival in New England. Pastor Brian Simmons, of Gateway Christian Fellowship in West Haven—at the time, one of the greatest prophetic revival churches in the whole Northeast—would hold major conferences and tell people, "I see him; he's coming. God is raising up a seventeen-year-old that He will use to see awakening in New England."

Dr. Simmons would urge people to get ready to be able to receive this person when he came. He would tell them that "the young man will have a bald head and tattoos." Just incredible!

At the same time God was telling people about who I was, here I was, hurting and believing God for a spiritual father. God blew away my wildest expectations! Throughout my life, He would bring me real spiritual fathers.

You may be reading this and already be in a place of having mentors like that. Stay close to them! Use those relationships for wisdom and guidance. Maybe, however, you are reading this and are just now in a place of realizing that you need spiritual fathers and mothers in your life. Just believe and stand on the promises of God. He hasn't forgotten you.

Fathers are needed today. As we realize that God uses family as a guide for our lives on earth, we can open ourselves up to what genuine fathering looks like. The truth is that we have all been hurt by leaders, especially spiritual ones. That doesn't take away from the real place of spiritual fathers in our lives. It is easy when we have been hurt to isolate ourselves or somehow believe that we can do it alone. That is a lie. We were meant to operate as a family.

God will use spiritual fathers to help us hear. And wisdom will be justified. Luke 7:35 (NKJV) says, "Wisdom is justified by all her children." This is so apparent today. Fathering is not supposed to be tyranny; it is not controlling. Fathering is guiding and loving, being compassionate and understanding, providing correction and being intentional in the relationship.

Don't Let the Recipe Die

Years ago, I had a friend whose grandfather cooked the greatest fish-and-chips you've ever had. No lie. He was a Portuguese fisherman in Connecticut, and they did stuff to fish that was incredible! They used cornmeal; that's all I know. We would go on Fridays and have fish. My mouth waters talking about it. It was just amazing. Despite everyone's best efforts, we knew that no one could cook fish like Grandpa could. Sadly, he died pretty young and unexpectedly. It was tragic. Still, the family wanted to get together one last time in his honor and even cook his famous fish-and-chips.

I remember driving up to the house and getting excited to have the famous dish one more time. Of course, we were all grieving, but this was an amazing bright spot in the day. I remember walking in, and something didn't smell right. I was taken aback, and as the evening went on, I took a glance at the fish that was coming out—trust me when I tell you it didn't look right! I was shocked. When I tasted it, it was even worse. Sadly, it tasted nothing like the fish-and-chips we knew. I went to one of Grandpa's kids and asked, "Who made this?"

This son told me, "Our oldest brother made it." Then he said, "I know it doesn't taste the same. . . . We never got the recipe."

I was shocked. With something so great, why hadn't the kids ever asked their dad for the recipe? I then began to hear the Lord speak to me about fathering. I am always honored, and I glean from the men of God before me, but what I realized in that moment is that we cannot let the recipes—the spiritual recipes—die with this generation of fathers and mothers. I was determined to unlock everything I could before these men and women of God passed.

It started with Dr. Brian Simmons, whom I just told you about. I gleaned everything I could from him. I asked him questions about the jungle in Panama, where he had spent years as a missionary and had translated the Bible into a language into which the Bible had never been translated. And I picked his brain until I began to think Kingdom.

Relationships are so important to God. God has given us relationships so we can thrive together. There is tremendous power in unity, in gathering together. Matthew 18:20 (NKJV) says, "Where two or three are gathered together in My name, I am there in the midst of them."

When Values Change, Relationships Change

Just as covenant relationships can help us thrive and hear God's voice, the opposite can happen when we have unhealthy relationships. I remember when I got saved, I was not spending time around the healthiest people. I was surrounded by friends who didn't share my values. I could never see my life without some of these people in it; these were long-term relationships I had. I was struggling with this, and when I was praying one day, I heard the Lord say to me, *When values change, relationships change.*

I was taken aback. Then I realized that God had entered my life, and as a result, this new value system wasn't going to fit with my old lifestyle. I still loved my friends; I still valued them. But it was time to move on. I changed my phone number and started believing God for new relationships. Relationships that had my value system. Connections that would pull me higher in God and not tear me down.

I have witnessed how prior relationships are a trap for so many Christians. We cannot value God's voice and be unaware of how the people we are around contribute to that—or don't. Are you around people who pull you higher? Are you spending time with people more spiritually mature than you? You will be like those you are around.

The Bible says in 1 Corinthians 15:33, "Do not be misled: 'Bad company corrupts good character.'" The company you keep will add to your relationship with Jesus, allowing you to grow, or it will hold you back. In this season, whom you are going into battle with is important. When you look to your left and to your right, whom do you see?

Proverbs 17:17 says, "A friend loves at all times, and a brother is born for a time of adversity." Who in your life is with you? Who is covenantally connected to you? I have noticed that in this Internet-driven world, few people have genuine covenant relationships. Somehow, today's connection leads to disconnection.

As we realize that God values relationships, we need to be prepared to believe for them and look for them. We need to seek out healthy relationships—true spiritual family who will encourage us to climb higher in God, and who will encourage us to continue maintaining a high standard of living in Him. No matter the cost.

Relationships Go through Seasons

We see in Psalm 41 that a close friend has turned against David:

> Even my close friend, someone I trusted, one who shared my bread, has turned against me.
>
> But may you have mercy on me, LORD; raise me up, that I may repay them. I know that you are pleased with me, for my enemy does not triumph over me. Because of my integrity you uphold me and set me in your presence forever.
>
> Praise be to the LORD, the God of Israel, from everlasting to everlasting. Amen and Amen.
>
> Psalm 41:9–13

There may be times when you will experience this kind of pain in your relationships. It is so important that we do not allow the hurt from past relationships to hinder us from experiencing healthy relationships. Otherwise, truthfully, we end up not trusting God when we get hurt.

I have had friends betray me. I have had people I work with and families we have opened up to completely turn and betray us. It has never changed my image of God or the value I place on relationships. It has opened me up to pray and forgive even more and to believe that God will replace these people and fill our lives with covenant relationships. And He has.

Also, we have seen relationships that disappeared, but then we reconnected with the same people many years later. When I was younger, it was one of my defense mechanisms to cut people off and shut them out. I had to do that when I got saved, as I said earlier, to protect the values in my new Christian lifestyle. As I got older and spiritually stronger, however, I began to have compassion for these relationships. They are all a treasure.

"He Will Need Your Shoulder . . ."

Many years ago, we had friends who served informally as pastors in our churches. One day, one of them sat down with me and shared his interest in planting a church. Of course I was excited, because I am absolutely called to plant churches and I am always excited when one of our leaders or pastors has a desire to launch out.

I immediately began to think of all the ways we could help our friends launch and fund a great church. Then my friend continued, "We don't want to plant an 'Engaging Heaven' church. We want to do our own thing."

This friend went on to thank us for our time together, but needless to say, that was a gut punch. It hurt for sure. I knew God was with us, however, and would work out exactly whom we needed to plant with. I basically washed my hands of it, blessed these friends and walked away from that meeting.

That night, I got a phone call from a very respected minister and prophet I knew. He called and asked me, "Are you okay?"

I told him I was, but I also told him that I had just had a weird meeting.

Then he said, "God showed me that one of your spiritual sons is trying to leave, and you are to let him go but stay close. It may be a few years, but he will need your shoulder again, and if you cut him off, he will not have the shoulder he needs to lean on."

I was speechless. I decided that night not to get offended and "cut off" this amazing couple. We decided that I would be here for whatever they needed. And just as the prophet said, a few years in, we started connecting again. My friend opened up, was honest, and asked if we would ordain him and pick up again where we left off. They wanted our covering and relationship. And trust me when I tell you it has been good. They purchased a new building after that talk, and they have a great church. And our relationship is stronger than it has ever been.

If I had not kept my heart clean and had not allowed God to soften my heart, I would have missed out on a great covenant relationship. We have to work on relationships and cultivate them. Just as we need to shed unhealthy ones, we will have to fight for the good ones. Misunderstanding is part of every relationship, but when you are all committed to a culture of honor, God will honor your relationships.

In fact, the strongest, healthiest, most fruitful relationships we have, have all been tried at some point. We have to be committed to keeping the great ones. I watch people all the time try to run from healthy relationships, and it just doesn't work. I see young people who despise fathering and spend years going in a circle spiritually, only to come around later.

Save your time now and realize the power that God has cultivated in healthy relationships. In Deuteronomy 32:30, the Bible tells us the power of covenant relationships: "How could one man chase a thousand, or two put ten thousand to flight, unless their Rock had sold them, unless the LORD had given them up?"

Read that again. It says *chase*. Did you see that? One person, isolated on his own, chases a thousand. That means it's exhausting, and nothing seems to work, and it's not filled with grace or peace. You are chasing, running in your own strength. However, just two . . . just two people put ten thousand to flight!

Association, Platform, Ministry

The fruit is in the cluster. It is the synergy and unity of relationships that allow God to move mightily. Years ago, long before I traveled the world, I was believing for greater things for ministry. There were three words God then gave me: *association, platform, ministry*.

The ministry wasn't the issue, and neither was the platform. I was already ministering to many people locally. The issue was association. I did not believe being part of a specific denomination would be helpful for me. I needed to believe for association.

Association wasn't hard, and it wasn't forced. It was a gradual building of relationships. Because of that, we have built strong relationships across the Body of Christ on many platforms and movements. We continue to build with ministries that burn for revival and reformation. Great fruit comes with the power of connection.

I believe that God is going to align you with the right covenant relationships that will catapult you into a new season of destiny and help place you where you are called to go. Nothing will hold you back. As the days get darker, God will connect you with true relationships that shine light and cultivate the prophetic in your life.

Prophetic Declaration and Prayer

Father, I thank You for every person reading this! I thank You that You value Kingdom connection, that You value covenant relationships. We decree and declare that this year, we will step into a greater connection with one another.

I thank You, Father, that real family is coming! Spiritual fathers and mothers full of faith and wisdom. I thank You that deep calls to deep, and that if there is a longing in our hearts for mentoring and fathering, You will fill it!

We give You praise in advance for the ten thousand being put to flight because of our association with others. As we cultivate Kingdom connection with one another, we will usher in a great awakening and an ability to hear You more clearly than ever before! We thank You for this, in Jesus' name! Amen.

Powerful Points about the Prophetic

- When it comes to the value of relationship, we all need human connection. We all long for it. We were designed to connect. With God, and with others.

- By far, one of the greatest needs I see today is spiritual fathering and mothering for a generation. Many people both young and old suffer today from a lack of mentoring.

- Instructors are needed, and honestly are everywhere. However, there are not many spiritual fathers. We have a fathering issue in Christianity.

- Fathering is not supposed to be tyranny; it is not controlling. Fathering is guiding and loving, being compassionate and understanding, providing correction and being intentional in the relationship.

- Relationships are so important to God. God has given us relationships so we can thrive together. There is tremendous power in unity, in gathering together.

- When values change, relationships change. We cannot value God's voice and be unaware of how the people we are around contribute to that—or don't.

- The company you keep will add to your relationship with Jesus, allowing you to grow, or it will hold you back.

- We need to seek out healthy relationships—true spiritual family who will encourage us to climb higher in God, and who will encourage us to continue maintaining a high standard of living in Him. No matter the cost.

- It is so important that we do not allow the hurt from past relationships to hinder us from experiencing healthy relationships. Otherwise, we end up not trusting God when we get hurt.

- We have to work on relationships and cultivate them. Just as we need to shed unhealthy ones, we will have to fight

for the good ones. Misunderstanding is part of every relationship, but when you are all committed to a culture of
honor, God will honor your relationships.

- The fruit is in the cluster. It is the synergy and unity of
  relationships that allow God to move mightily. Great fruit
  comes with the power of connection.
- As the days get darker, God will connect you and me with
  true relationships that shine light and cultivate the prophetic in our lives.

7

HEARING WITH CONFIDENCE

The Value of Loving the Written Word of God

God has given us a gift on this earth. It is the gift of the Word of God. Imagine with me for a moment living in Bible days and walking in the footsteps of Jesus, where you encountered God and walked in power and authority. The most mind-blowing thought is the fact that we have the written Word of God, and the early believers did not!

Let that sink in. The early Church was writing the story of the Gospel, learning about Jesus and His ways, obeying Him and writing about their experiences. They walked in power, preached the Gospel and served God without a full Bible.

Jesus loves us so much that He died on the cross and relegated all power and authority to us. He also gave us the inspired Word of God. This Word, which is "sharper than any two-edged sword" (Hebrews 4:12 NKJV), is a roadmap to relationship with God that will guide our lives forever. It is the guidebook in which life flows. It is an anchor for us and a foundation for our every experience. If we are going to hear from God clearly, we must develop a love for the written Word of God.

Current and Constant

The Holy Bible was written by people of God who encountered Him. They walked in and witnessed miracles; they overcame adversity and saw cities and regions shaken. The authors didn't write the Bible as a history book alone. It was never meant to be some sort of clinical study. This was a book that was meant to be unlocked by passionate lovers. There was a Presence involved when it was written. When and if pursued and tapped into, this Presence would allow the Word of God to come alive and transform the lives of families and churches.

We have the Bible—the written Word that is the constant Word. We also have the current, daily prophetic word—the guiding words of God through faithful human vessels. God desires that we listen to both.

Jesus would say, "He who has ears to hear, let him hear!" (Matthew 11:15 NKJV). That means we can read but not hear. That means we can recite yet not tap in. There are two ways to read the Word: with or without the Holy Spirit. Reading with the Holy Spirit produces results. This was how we were meant to live. Through the reading of the Word, we create space to allow God to visit and speak to us. The Bible is clear when it says, "Faith comes by hearing, and hearing by the word of God" (Romans 10:17 NKJV).

Did you see that? Faith doesn't come by having heard. Faith comes by hearing, and one of the ways God will continually speak to us is through His Word. We cannot read the Bible in our flesh as if it's a history book and expect to get results. It won't happen. It will end up being used as a control tool to hurt others, and when used improperly, it can cause great pain and division. We must tap into the Spirit and the relationship in which it was written. Faith comes this way. That is how it was always meant to be.

When properly read and devoured, the Bible can set captives free. This Book can allow Jesus to flood your life and transform you forever. I remember as a young believer, I looked at all the Christians around me and honestly didn't feel adequate. I came from a broken home, drugs and a rough background. No one in my family was born again. I never knew God. And looking at all of these families in the church, I simply didn't feel good enough to be used by God one day.

Then I started reading the Bible. Wow! My life was changed forever. And through marking so many Scriptures with multiple highlighters and using my pen to underline all the Scriptures that stuck out, my life was transformed.

I remember reading Psalm 107:20 (NKJV), "He sent his word and healed them, and delivered them from their destructions." I realized this Word was made flesh: "In the beginning was the Word . . . and the Word became flesh and dwelt among us" (John 1:1, 14 NKJV). This message of the Gospel was not just for the rich and put-together; this Gospel was for me!

I was also reminded, "But God chose the foolish things of the world to shame the wise; God chose the weak things of the world to shame the strong" (1 Corinthians 1:27).

Through these and many other Scriptures, I began to believe. Faith flooded my heart. God started speaking to me through His Word, and He began to speak to me in my heart. I would then read the Scriptures and see miracles. I would see the dead raised, I would see sight restored to the blind and hearing restored to the deaf, and I realized there is nothing that God cannot do! The Word enhanced my desire for experiences and visitation. I developed a hunger for the Word, and a hunger to experience the God of the Word. That is the bottom line of it all.

Bible knowledge without Bible experience is pointless. Paul echoed this in Romans 15:19 (NKJV) when he said that with "mighty signs and wonders, by the power of the Spirit of God . . . I have fully preached the gospel of Christ." Paul said fully preaching the Gospel was preaching with mighty signs and wonders. Let that sink in! It's about time we start becoming full-gospel people. A half gospel won't work.

I Don't Believe That

A few years ago, I was interviewed by Sid Roth for my previous book *Fire! Preparing for the Next Great Holy Spirit Outpouring* (Chosen, 2019). I was excited for the opportunity. There have been many accurate prophets and men and women of God on Sid's show, *It's Supernatural!* As we were preparing, we were talking about some of the radical miracles we have seen—a baby raised from the dead, people's arms growing out, eyes being formed. In over twenty years of traveling and pastoring, you see a few things. Again, my interview contained some amazing stories, but these weren't everyday stories. These were some amazing highlights from twenty years of pursuing God.[1]

When the interview launched, I was amazed that so many people did not believe that radical miracles could happen. Just a few weeks ago, someone approached me at one of our churches and said, "Pastor, I just watched your interview with Sid Roth. You were talking about being translated in prayer to India and helping people in a tsunami. . . ." Then

107

he said, "I just can't believe that." He wasn't attacking me or being critical; he was being honest. It was just too crazy for him to comprehend. Yet it is possible for what God has done before to happen again, even if we don't make these unusual manifestations our focus (see Acts 8:39–40, where Philip was translated).

What I said to him is what I say many times when people don't understand something: "I understand. However, it's in the Bible, you know."

We are at a point when even if it's in the Bible, we don't have a grid for it. Simply because we don't see and experience these things often, we dismiss them as unbelievable because we don't understand them. Thankfully, I know men and women all over this earth who have experienced similar things, and far more than I have. I've seen just a couple of people raised from the dead, but I have ministers close to me in the faith who have seen five hundred raisings! I would never allow myself to be blinded because I don't understand something.

The Word of God has opened up my life to continue to pursue Jesus and stand on His Word. Whatever we face in life, seen or unseen, the Word has an answer for us. This is the plan of heaven: that we would devour the Word, stand on it and continue to experience what the Bible mentions we can have. We cannot approach the supernatural with doubt and unbelief. If we truly have a relationship with Jesus, then reading and devouring the Word of God will result in our demonstrating greater measures of faith.

Hindering Your Hearing and Seeing

Just as it's possible to read the Word and doubt miracles and experiences, we also can hinder our hearing and seeing by

reading the Word wrong. That's why there are denominations today that love God but completely dismiss miracles.
Now, you may think charismatics would never get that way,
but I can see it happening. We are called to live and walk in
revival, according to God's Word.

David summed it up best:

> My soul clings to the dust; revive me according to Your word.
> I have declared my ways, and You answered me; teach me
> Your statutes. Make me understand the way of Your pre-
> cepts; so shall I meditate on your wonderful works.
>
> Psalm 119:25–27 NKJV

This is the cry of a revived heart.

If you are a pastor, you realize that it's a very high calling.
It's something you cannot take lightly; the Bible even says
that we will be judged harder (see James 3:1). There is nothing more heartbreaking than having people lead the saints
of God if those leaders aren't revived or walking in power.
The blind cannot lead the blind. We need apostles, prophets
and evangelists who walk in the power of the Word and have
renewed their minds by the Word of God.

I once attended a conference in another country. I was one
of several conference speakers that weekend, some of whom
I looked up to. We were doing a tent crusade outside. It was
awesome. All the speakers stayed at a local hotel, and we were
transported together on a bus to and from the meetings. It
was a great fellowship and bonding time.

On the second night, as my friend who was hosting the
conference was receiving the offering, one of the outside
vendors tapped me on the shoulder and said there was an
emergency. (There were booths and food trucks outside the
tent.) A man had collapsed outside and needed help. As

soon as I heard that, I slipped out of the meeting and went outside. I saw a guy on the ground, and he was in pain. He looked at me and in complete despair said, "This is it! I'm going to die."

They told me this man had only one kidney, and the one he had was bad. He was on dialysis daily, and it was a matter of time before the dialysis wouldn't work anymore and he would die. I honestly didn't think twice about what I did next, because I realize there are no accidents in life, only divine appointments. I looked at him and said, "You will not die! God is going to give you a new kidney!"

We began to pray. We cursed every attack, and we commanded a new kidney to be given to him. He immediately got up and said the pain had left. We rejoiced and clapped for joy!

I quickly went back to the meeting. As I sat down, one of the ministers leaned over to me. "What happened out there?" he asked.

"There was an emergency, and we prayed, and God just gave this guy a new kidney!" I testified.

"Really?" he said as he leaned back over in his chair.

I didn't think anything of it. After a powerful meeting, full of many miracles, we headed back to the bus. The same minister who asked me what happened out there sat next to me.

"Hey, man," he said, "that testimony you shared about the kidney—you should be careful about saying that." He added, "Especially if you don't know."

I was taken aback by the conversation. "I am sure, bro," I said. "We prayed for a new kidney, and he jumped up with no pain. Should I assume he's still sick?" I sarcastically said.

We agreed to let it go. However, the next day was wild! As we were pulling up, there was a crowd of people in the streets around the tent. Something was happening. When we got off the bus, I saw the man who had collapsed the night before. This time, he was surrounded by a group of people! He ran up to me and told me how he got up after we prayed and he urinated with no pain. He then went to the doctor and told the doctor what had happened. Then this man pulled out two X-rays to show me. One was from a few weeks ago, showing one kidney that was failing in his body. The other, an X-ray from this very day, showed his failing kidney restored *and a new kidney that had grown in his body.*

Yes, one kidney was restored and another kidney grew back—for a total of two! This was incredible!

The minister who tried to correct me? He apologized, saying that he wanted to read the Word of God with greater faith and hear God clearly. Of course, I loved on him and honored him. However, I walked away and realized that if insiders are struggling to hear and have faith, then how much more important is it that we as the people of God must stay in the Word?

The Word Is Alive

Hebrews 4:12 (NKJV) tells us, "For the word of God is living and powerful, and sharper than any two-edged sword, piercing even to the division of soul and spirit, and of joints and marrow, and is a discerner of the thoughts and intents of the heart."

The Word is alive! It's active! The devil wants nothing more than for the Word to be stale and dead to you, appearing void of power. The devil is telling a generation that unholy is holy, and that evil is good. We need the Word of God as a standard on how to live. The Word is a huge prophetic key for walking in the supernatural. We have to know what has been made available to us. That means truth is truth. It is not subjective; it is truth. It is not open for debate; it is truth. Even if it is not popular, it doesn't take away from the fact that it is truth.

Jesus prays to the Father in John 17:17 (NKJV), "Sanctify them by Your truth. Your word is truth." We have an obligation as a prophetic company to hold truth. Even guard it!

Paul told Timothy, "O Timothy! Guard what was committed to your trust, avoiding the profane and idle babblings and contradictions of what is falsely called knowledge" (1 Timothy 6:20 NKJV). We are one generation away from removing biblical truth from this earth if we do not lean into the Word and begin to experience God and believe.

I have watched "science" creep into the Church, with false knowledge slipping in. We have spent more time counseling demons than casting them out. We make room for mental health issues without cursing the demons at the root of some of these and breaking people's torment. Somehow, we think it's love. It's not; it's compromise. We must respond to every sickness and disease the way Jesus did. We are people who believe in the full Gospel. The Word is alive!

"We Are a Church; We Believe in Jesus."

Shortly after we purchased our amazing church building in New London, Connecticut, we realized the church was being used for community programs every night of the week. At first I didn't mind, especially if people were paying. We were an inner-city church that feeds the homeless daily, and the extra rent would be helpful. Except when I looked at the records, I realized that the community users had never paid rent. Like, never.

I approached each of the groups, which were various drug and alcohol rehab programs, 12-Step stuff. Again, I didn't mind their meeting in the church, but they were going to pay or I would simply kick them out. Well, after many warnings I kicked all of them out—except one Alcoholics Anonymous group.

Right around that time, there was a bad batch of heroin that came through the city, and many people were dying. It wasn't good timing. I started being attacked for canceling the programs, as if I had contributed to these addicts' deaths. Multiple requests came in for interviews to talk about it, but I didn't do any. Then our local paper approached me to do a story on the drug pandemic and what the area pastors' response should be. I agreed to meet. In fact, I called back everyone who had wanted an interview and decided to do one larger interview in my office. TV crews and newspaper representatives all gathered there, and I was ready for them.

"I would like to thank you all for coming," I opened, and quickly got to the point. "I want to apologize to all of you now. I misled you. We are not a community organization. We are not a community center. We are a church. And I do not believe you can get freedom outside of Jesus Christ."

I told them that with all the ex–drug addicts we worked with, we saw a 100 percent success rate with Jesus. The Word of God was our program, and with encountering Jesus, these people would never go back to the addictions again. I offered to clear the front row of the church for anyone addicted to drugs and alcohol to come and experience God. It was a major moment for us and for the city. The best part is that we saw people come get delivered through the invitation.

This world is hurting and is looking for solutions. People need to know what the Lord says about them. We must develop a love for the Word of God and position ourselves to hear Him and to walk in greater power. When Jesus was tempted, He used the Word. The Bible is filled with life for you and me. David said, "I have hidden your word in my heart that I might not sin against you" (Psalm 119:11).

The Word will cleanse you. It will be a weapon against the devil. It will be strength to your body. We must read and believe. I encourage you today to find a daily devotional to help you dive into the Word of God every day. Of course, I recommend our daily devotional *Engaging Heaven Today: 365 Daily Devotionals* (Broadstreet, 2022). You can read it each day, and I believe it will ignite your faith. As I mentioned earlier, we also have a daily podcast, *Engage Heaven with James Levesque*, so every day we hear a fresh word from God. Get ready!

Prophetic Declaration and Prayer

God is going to renew your love for the Word, and you will begin to see revelation like never before. Fresh wisdom is going to fall on you. As you read and devour the Word, you will begin to hear God's voice clearly. You will begin to prophesy in accordance with the written and constant Word of God.

Father, we thank You for Your Word. Today, I pray for every person reading this. I pray a fresh love for the Word would spark in our hearts. I declare this will be the year, through Your Word, that we hear Your voice more clearly than ever before.

I declare a renewed mind for each of us, filled with wisdom and revelation in the knowledge of You! We thank You now for a fresh presence around this Word, and I prophesy that biblical encounters await each of us reading these words! It's time to ascend to the heavenly realms, in Jesus' name! Amen.

Powerful Points about the Prophetic

- There is great value in loving the written Word of God. If we are going to hear from God clearly, we must develop a love for His written Word.
- There are two ways to read the Word: with or without the Holy Spirit. Reading with the Holy Spirit produces results. This was how we were meant to live.
- Bible knowledge without Bible experience is pointless. It's about time we start becoming full-gospel people. A half gospel won't work.
- This is the plan of heaven: that we would devour the Word, stand on it and continue to experience what the Bible mentions we can have.
- We cannot approach the supernatural with doubt and unbelief. If we truly have a relationship with Jesus, then reading and devouring the Word of God will result in our demonstrating greater measures of faith.
- Just as it's possible to read the Word and doubt miracles and experiences, we also can hinder our hearing and seeing by reading the Word wrong. We are called to live and walk in revival, according to God's Word.
- The Word of God is a huge prophetic key for walking in the supernatural. We have to know what has been made available to us.
- We are one generation away from removing biblical truth from this earth if we do not lean into the Word and begin to experience God and believe.
- We must respond to every sickness and disease the way Jesus did. We are people who believe in the full Gospel. The Word is alive!
- This world is hurting and is looking for solutions. People need to know what the Lord says about them.

- We must develop a love for the Word of God and position ourselves to hear and to walk in greater power. When Jesus was tempted, He used the Word. The Bible is filled with life for you and me.
- The Word will cleanse you. It will be a weapon against the devil. It will be strength to your body. We must read and believe.

8

THE ANCHOR
OF HOPE

The Value of Endless Hope

Hope. If there was ever a day when we need endless hope, it is today. We are living in a day where so many are struggling for hope. Hope for the future, hope for family, hope within the Church. The beautiful thing is, with Jesus we have all hope!

What if I told you that your ability to connect with God is directly connected to your level of hope? We have all seen our share of cranky prophets, people of doom who allow their unbelief and anger to spill out in all they say. That is not hope. We are about to see prophets of hope arise with mighty signs and wonders.

● Biblical Hope versus Earthly Hope

The book of Romans gives us an amazing insight into hope. Here is what I believe is one of the greatest Scriptures on hope:

> . . . in the presence of Him who he [Abraham] believed—
> God, who gives life to the dead and calls those things which
> do not exist as though they did; who, contrary to hope,
> in hope believed, so that he became the father of many
> nations.
>
> Romans 4:17–18 NKJV

This is powerful. Abraham, against all hope, in hope believed! How is that even possible? How can you, in the face of earthly hopelessness, have hope? It is because earthly hope and Kingdom hope are vastly different. When you have hope on this earth, consider it nothing more than a wish. It's like saying, "I hope it doesn't rain this weekend." That's not actually faith-filled; it's an earthly wish that may or may not happen. In the natural, the future has no divine connection; it's a gamble. Yet the Bible says that in the face of earthly wishing, Abraham had biblical hope.

The definition of *hope* in the Bible is a joyful anticipation of good (see 2 Corinthians 1:7 AMPC). Kingdom hope doesn't end. Kingdom hope gives us a peace always, and a great anticipation of things to come.

What you behold, you become. Our thoughts and our lives are connected to hope. What we speak is connected to hope. Hope is the value that keeps our hearing of the voice of God pure. We control the flow of our hearing, and what our spirits pick up and believe will determine what happens around us.

The Bible reminds us that "the spirits of the prophets are subject to the prophets" (1 Corinthians 14:32 NKJV). That's good and bad. Any prophetic word that comes from God through us requires that we have hope, or else we won't be able to prophesy correctly. What are your beliefs? How has hope allowed you to have a greater future and promise?

● COVID-19 and the U.S. Elections

The year 2020 was one of the craziest years of our lives, ever. Going into it, we didn't have any real warning, just some simple prophetic words about seeing clearly and "2020" vision. Then most people's worlds got flipped. Add isolation, lockdowns, masks and vaccines, and we watched so many Christians be destroyed. I never could have imagined it. At the same time, it was an American election year, with a result that most of the Church wasn't ready for. And Christians in other nations faced huge challenges of their own. The challenge of these setbacks is that whatever is inside you when they happen will come out.

Storms come and go; Jesus does not. Mark 4:36 (NKJV) tells us something interesting about Jesus and storms: "Now when they had left the multitude, they took Him along in the boat as He was."

Did you catch that? *As He was* to them. When seasons of difficulty come, you will become more of what you already are. Or should I say Jesus will become more of who He is to you at the time? If Jesus has your complete trust during a difficult season, then any shake-up just redefines what you already believed.

If people's complete trust isn't in Jesus during difficult seasons, or if they don't believe in healing, then an event like the pandemic becomes a failed fire drill, a missed opportunity. Fear became the real disease for many people in 2020, and it wasn't political; it was biblical.

What we thought was the state of the Church was flipped upside down during that time, and it wasn't great. I can tell you, as I'm writing this book beyond 2020, that we still have people who have not come back to church! When they got into the boat, Jesus wasn't their protector. They didn't have hope. There wasn't a joy that God was working all things out. If you struggled to believe God was your provider before, your struggle only got worse in the storms. If you struggled to be hope filled, it showed. The time frame starting with 2020 exposed believers' shaky foundations in a way I've never witnessed. Even the prophetic movement seemed to be on life support.

What was God speaking through all of this? I know He is moving. We will see the prophetic movement fully restored on this earth. These temporary shake-ups will make you and me stronger. Now is the time to believe. This is the greatest hour we have ever lived in!

Hope as an Anchor

When 2020 began, I was living in Connecticut. COVID-19 mandates started going into effect, and businesses and churches started shutting down. At that time, I declared it would be the greatest year of our lives. I declared the ministry would expand, and I declared the churches would grow and lives would be saved, delivered and healed! I knew beyond a shadow of doubt the Jesus who was getting into our boats. We would only advance! I had great hope.

That hope wasn't birthed from a place of fear or earthly wishing. I truly believed that hidden in this battle was promotion. However, we had to believe. We had to link to our anchor. Hebrews 6:19–20 tells us that He is the anchor of our hope: "We have this hope as an anchor for the soul, firm and secure. It enters the inner sanctuary behind the curtain, where our forerunner, Jesus, has entered on our behalf."

Here in Florida, where we live now, there are many boats. I had never driven a boat until I moved here. However, I recently had to take an eight-hour course on boating to get a license. I learned a lot about anchors. One definition of the word *anchor* is "a heavy device that is attached to a boat or ship by a rope or chain and that is thrown into the water to hold the boat or ship in place."[1]

Jesus is our anchor. And what about our hope? We just saw that the Bible talks about hope as an anchor. That means no matter what we go through, our boat doesn't move. That means when the winds and waves crash against us, we will not be moved. If we truly have hope, then our anchor has been Jesus. I am telling you, when you have hope—real hope, biblical hope—you will not be moved.

In 2020, I knew we would not be moved. We saw churches close down and never open again. Yet I knew God would not only sustain us, but also increase us in ways we could never have imagined. As we declared that 2020 would be the greatest year we ever had, that's what it became. By December 2020, we were purchasing our property to plant our Madeira Beach, Florida, location. Our churches in Connecticut and Montana were growing, and lives were being transformed. We also ordained and covered another five churches that year.

I am telling you, our God is the God of miracles. Jesus is our hope! We have seen God's hand move more in the past few years than ever before. And I am also telling you, this will be your greatest year yet! It is time to believe and walk in His promises.

Sick Hearts and Trusting

What happens when you have believed and hoped for something, and it hasn't happened? First of all, it will happen, in Jesus' name! Second, when hope seems deferred, it can cause pain. The Bible tells us, "Hope deferred makes the heart sick, but when the desire comes, it is a tree of life" (Proverbs 13:12 NKJV). We need to understand that and not get stuck in the pain while we wait, because life is coming.

A lot of people are living with sick hearts. There is a direct connection between hope and our hearts, and between hope and our joy. Your hope level is connected to your ability to realize the promises of God. Years ago, I was believing for some things that had not happened. It was a discouraging time. I felt as though a few promises should have been fulfilled by that point. You know how we put a timeline on God? I felt that I knew when God was going to do something, yet it hadn't happened.

Hope deferred makes the heart sick. But when desire is realized, when we realize what heaven has, when we realize what God has said, it becomes a tree of life inside us. That is the power of hope. I don't believe you need to let any hopelessness come into your life. I believe we can live in the place of the tree of life. Realizing God's promises means that we remember the promises and stay in the Word, standing on Him!

One day in prayer, I was asking the Lord about some prophetic words and promises that hadn't come to pass. I knew God had spoken to me about them, and I couldn't understand why these things hadn't happened. As I was praying, I heard the Lord speak very clearly to me: *I give you the promise (seed); you give the trust.*

This really impacted me. I believe the promises of God are always connected to a life-giving tree. Why? Because every promise starts with a seed. God is not asking us to understand. He is asking us to trust. He gives the seed; we give the trust, the faithfulness. That's our partnership.

The next morning was a Sunday. As I woke up excited for a full day of services, God spoke again and said, *I want you to trust Me beyond your level of understanding.*

When I heard that, I immediately remembered Proverbs 3:1–8:

> My son, do not forget my teaching, but keep my commands in your heart, for they will prolong your life many years and bring you peace and prosperity.
>
> Let love and faithfulness never leave you; bind them around your neck, write them on the tablet of your heart. Then you will win favor and a good name in the sight of God and man.
>
> Trust in the LORD with all your heart and lean not on your own understanding; in all your ways submit to him, and he will make your paths straight.
>
> Do not be wise in your own eyes; fear the LORD and shun evil. This will bring health to your body and nourishment to your bones.

We see here so many promises for us. God commands us not to trust in our own understanding. That means do not let your trust be that which supports you. It is so tempting to step into the place of reason. Do not commit "reason treason"! Our natural mind will always be at war with God, and it will steal our hope. We must stay with a supernatural mind. Understanding can come in the form of wisdom and revelation, or understanding can come supernaturally, through discernment. It also can come through the flesh and be a hindrance to us. It is so easy when we feel discouraged to lean on our own thoughts and understanding.

Hope and trust are eternally connected. I want to expound on this a bit more. Matthew 16:21–23 (NKJV) shows the disciples facing a difficult time. Jesus was going to leave eventually, and the word was getting out. The disciples loved Jesus and didn't understand why or even how the terrible things ahead would happen. Naturally, they didn't want Him to die:

> From that time Jesus began to show to His disciples that He must go to Jerusalem, and suffer many things from the elders and chief priests and scribes, and be killed, and be raised the third day.
>
> Then Peter took Him aside and began to rebuke Him, saying, "Far be it from You, Lord; this shall not happen to You!"
>
> But He turned and said to Peter, "Get behind Me, Satan! You are an offense to Me, for you are not mindful of the things of God, but the things of men.

This is wild! Right before this, Peter had made the famous "You are the Christ" declaration (verse 16). And right before this, Jesus had also told them not to tell anyone who He was (see verse 20). Jesus was prolonging His life by giving them this command because He realized that the disciples had finally realized who He was. He was the Messiah!

Peter didn't understand what was happening. He thought he was being loyal, faithful Peter. He thought he was protecting Jesus; he just didn't understand. Peter started leaning on his own understanding. Earthly logic was telling him they needed to protect Jesus and not let Him die. However, Peter's earthly logic would literally have gone against God's plan. So much so, that Jesus said, "Get behind Me, Satan!"

That's intense! Jesus didn't believe Peter was the devil. Instead, He saw the devil's plans in Peter's natural mind. Jesus knew that when we think naturally, it can allow "sick hearts" to prevail. This tells me that when we lean on our own understanding, it opens the door for demonic influence in our lives. We are entering a moment in time when we have to live in the "desire realized" side of hope. We must stand on God's Word and on His prophetic words, and then watch Him promote and increase our lives!

We Must Remember

It is important that we remember the Word of the Lord. Proverbs 3:1–2 says, "My son, do not forget my teaching, but keep my commands in your heart, for they will prolong your life many years and bring you peace and prosperity."

The Bible is filled with reminders not to forget God's promises. Forgetting His promises will steal hope and cause a sick state in your heart. The Lord commands us not to forget. And not only not to forget, but to keep His words in our hearts. Our hearts. The same place that becomes "sick" with hopelessness. Our hearts must be guarded and protected so we can walk in God's promises. The reason the Bible continually tells us not to forget is because it is easy to forget.

We know the Israelites saw miracles. However, they would drink from the river and die in the wilderness. Seems crazy, right? The Bible gives us insight into how a generation can experience such deliverance and yet perish: "Then they believed His words; they sang His praise. They soon *forgot* His works; they did not wait for His counsel, but lusted exceedingly in the wilderness, and tested God in the desert" (Psalm 106:12–14 NKJV, emphasis added).

That's how the people died. Although they saw miracles and drank from the river, in the end, they forgot God's works. It is so easy to be overcome by hopelessness that we forget. And forgetting is the sick part. Forgetting is the place of denying promise. We must never forget.

Anytime my wife, Debbie, and I speak with a person or a couple going through difficulties, real trauma in which they seem to have no hope, I immediately tell them, "Write a list." I have stood over parents who lost children; I have stood over people about to get locked up for many years. It doesn't matter; they must write a list of the things God has done for them that they are thankful for.

We all need to write a list. Why? Because we need to be reminded of all that God has done. If "forgetting" causes death, "remembering" brings life!

We all have so much to be thankful for, and thanksgiving opens the door to hope. I want to encourage you to write a list. No matter what you are facing or believing for, write a list. Start to list all the things God has done for you that you are thankful for. We have so much to be grateful for. As we keep thanksgiving on our lips, heaven will move on our behalf.

Endless Hope on the Horizon

What should our posture be? How can we position ourselves to continue living in endless hope? There is a prophetic story in the Bible that I believe gives us keys to unlocking endless hope:

> And Elijah said to Ahab, "Go, eat and drink, for there is the sound of a heavy rain." So Ahab went off to eat and drink, but Elijah climbed to the top of Carmel, bent down to the ground and put his face between his knees.
>
> "Go and look toward the sea," he told his servant. And he went up and looked.
>
> "There is nothing there," he said.
>
> Seven times Elijah said, "Go back."

The seventh time the servant reported, "A cloud as small as a man's hand is rising from the sea."

So Elijah said, "Go and tell Ahab, 'Hitch up your chariot and go down before the rain stops you.'"

Meanwhile, the sky grew black with clouds, the wind rose, a heavy rain started falling and Ahab rode off to Jezreel. The power of the LORD came on Elijah and, tucking his cloak into his belt, he ran ahead of Ahab all the way to Jezreel.

1 Kings 18:41–46

There was a drought in the land. They needed rain to fall, they needed God to invade, they needed hope. Immediately, the prophet Elijah gets in what is almost a fetal position, because he hears the sound of an abundance of rain. There wasn't any rain, just a promise of rain, and now he could hear it. When we link to our anchor in faith, stand on God's promises and remember His goodness, we are positioned to receive the abundance of rain.

Elijah tells his servant to go look and see if there is any rain on the horizon. Can you imagine the excitement? I would have been running toward the sea! Can you imagine waiting for the drought to end? Everyone had been waiting for this moment. Remember, God had promised them it would end. They need a sign, and then the prophet hears the sound. This is amazing! I would have run as fast as I could to see the rain.

And then, it wasn't there.

His servant comes back to tell him, "There is nothing there."

This is the moment of decision. What do you believe? Do you believe that God spoke, or do you believe the drought you see? The prophet saw a cloud, but the servant only saw a sky without clouds. That could have been discouraging. But thank God for prophets of hope!

"Go back," Elijah said.

And the next time, there is no sign of rain, and the next, and the next. Six times, Elijah's servant looks to the sea but can't see a sign. I'm not sure I know many people who would do that six times. I have people who don't come to church because one time they couldn't find a parking spot! Never mind six times. Six. That's discouraging. But thank God for the seventh time!

The seventh time, the servant sees something: "A cloud as small as a man's hand is rising from the sea." Thank You, Lord. God delivered them from a drought with that trip.

I feel the Lord speaking right now, and He is asking, *Are you willing to live with a cloudless sky?*

Are we willing to have endless hope, despite not seeing the promise yet? I am telling you, keep looking! God gives the promise; we give the trust. We do not have to understand, but we have to keep looking on the horizon.

Prophetic Declaration and Prayer

I am telling you that as I write this, I feel heaven so strongly, and I prophesy to you that this is the year the drought ends! This is the year you see the hand of heaven move on your family and your church. This is the year that God's glory invades your life!

Father, I thank You that today we are being surged with endless hope! Lord, we thank You that You are a faithful God. You are a worthy God who has deposited promises in our lives. We know that You began a good work in us, and You are faithful.

Jesus, we thank You that this is the year when long battles will come to an end. This is the year when we will see the cloud! This is the year when the rain of heaven will fall on our homes, schools, churches, cities, regions, nations, the world! In the mighty name of Jesus! Amen.

Powerful Points about the Prophetic

- If there was ever a day when we need endless hope, it is today. We are living in a day where so many are struggling for hope. With Jesus, we have all hope!

- The definition of *hope* in the Bible is a joyful anticipation of good (see 2 Corinthians 1:7 AMPC). Kingdom hope doesn't end. Kingdom hope gives us a peace always, and a great anticipation of things to come.

- Hope is the value that keeps our hearing of the voice of God pure. We control the flow of our hearing, and what our spirits pick up and believe will determine what happens around us.

- Storms come and go; Jesus does not. When seasons of difficulty come, Jesus will become more of who He is to you at the time. If Jesus has your complete trust during a difficult season, then any shake-up just redefines what you already believed.

- Jesus is our anchor. And the Bible talks about hope as an anchor. That means no matter what we go through, our boat doesn't move. When the winds and waves crash against us, we will not be moved.

- Proverbs 13:12 (NKJV) tells us, "Hope deferred makes the heart sick, but when the desire comes, it is a tree of life." We need to understand that and not get stuck in the pain while we wait, because life is coming.

- There is a direct connection between hope and our hearts, and between hope and our joy. Your hope level is connected to your ability to realize the promises of God.

- I heard the Lord speak very clearly to me: *I give you the promise (seed); you give the trust.* Every promise starts with a seed.

- God is not asking us to understand. He is asking us to trust. He gives the seed; we give the trust, the faithfulness. That's our partnership.

- God spoke again and said, *I want you to trust Me beyond your level of understanding.* It is so easy when we feel discouraged to lean on our own thoughts and understanding, but He commands us not to trust in our own understanding.

- It is so tempting to step into the place of reason. Do not commit "reason treason"! Our natural mind will always be at war with God, and it will steal our hope. We must stay with a supernatural mind.

- Forgetting God's promises will steal hope and cause a sick state in your heart. The Lord commands us not to forget. We need to be reminded of all that God has done. If "forgetting" causes death, "remembering" brings life!

- We all have so much to be thankful for, and thanksgiving opens the door to hope. As we keep thanksgiving on our lips, heaven will move on our behalf.

- Are we willing to have endless hope, despite not seeing the promise yet? Keep looking! God gives the promise; we give the trust. We do not have to understand, but we have to keep looking on the horizon.

9

REDISCOVERING THE KINGDOM

The Value of Knowing What We Have Been Given

I was at a conference and participating in a panel discussion when someone asked me, "Pastor James, what do you think is the greatest hindrance to Christianity today?"

I thought this was a great question, and it came from a pure heart. After a quick thought, I boldly answered, "I believe the greatest hindrance to Christianity today is a lack of knowledge about what we've been given."

We have been pressed by our lack of knowledge about what is available. First Corinthians 2:12 (NKJV) says, "Now we have received, not the spirit of the world, but the Spirit who is from God, that we might know the things that have been freely given to us by God." We have to know.

When I was born again, I was desperate for God. No one in my family was born again, and I had just encountered Jesus so powerfully. It produced a deep longing to know all that the Kingdom has made available. I quickly realized the religious system I first experienced was not set up for me—a poor kid from the projects who had just met God and instantly had a passion and love for Him. The structure was boards, deacons, elders and families who gave a lot of money. It is easy within that structure to find yourself trying to please people for some church recognition rather than encountering God and receiving His Kingdom.

One Wednesday night during a predictable pause in worship, a message of tongues and interpretation came forth. I was so desperate to hear God speak that I fell on my face and started weeping. The thought of God in the room was frightening. *God is actually speaking!* I thought to myself.

"*Worship Me*, says the Lord. *Worship Me . . . kneel before your Maker*," the interpreter of the tongues said. The challenge for me was that when I looked around the room, no one was kneeling. Umm . . . no one was even praying. The pastor quickly prayed, and suddenly we were doing the announcements. Awkwardly, I was still on the ground; clearly, I hadn't understood the assignment.

There Must Be More

I got up and left out the back after that service, so upset. How could God's voice and the gifts be reduced to a predictable, unanointed routine? Why are we saying that God is speaking, if I don't see or feel Jesus in the room?

Despite a youth pastor trying to convince me that what had happened was okay, I was not okay with it. I knew that the Jesus who had encountered me in my mom's house, the

God of fire, was not allowed to manifest in that place. I didn't trash church after that, but I gave my life to seeing presence-driven churches established all across this land.

One Sunday a few weeks before that Wednesday night, I found myself leaving church feeling empty inside. I left church discouraged and decided to go to the ocean. There, I began to cry out to Him. I remember walking on the rocks, looking at the ocean and screaming, *God, where are You?! Is this all I get for the week?* And then as a new believer so desperate for Him, I screamed, *God! I gave up sex and drugs for this?*

I just knew that there was so much more for me. Right then, a plastic Dixie cup washed up on the rocks where I was seated. As I stared at it, I was reminded of a Kathryn Kuhlman quote. (When I was born again, I devoured everything I could on Spirit-filled Christianity.) I could hear her in my ear, speaking, "We're asking for a cupful and the ocean remains."[1] Why do we settle for a cupful, when the whole ocean is ours? As tears were falling down my face, I was resolved never to go back to dead religion again.

Our Mandate

In the book of Matthew, Jesus gave us a commission, although many do not realize it:

> And when you pray, do not be like the hypocrites, for they love to pray standing in the synagogues and on the street corners to be seen by others. Truly I tell you, they have received their reward in full. But when you pray, go into your room, close the door and pray to your Father, who is unseen. Then your Father, who sees what is done in secret, will reward you. And when you pray, do not keep on babbling like pagans, for

they think they will be heard because of their many words. Do not be like them, for your Father knows what you need before you ask him.

This, then, is how you should pray:

"Our Father in heaven, hallowed be your name, your kingdom come, your will be done, on earth as it is in heaven. Give us today our daily bread. And forgive us our debts, as we also have forgiven our debtors. And lead us not into temptation, but deliver us from the evil one."

Matthew 6:5–13

As it is in heaven. This is our mandate. As important as the Great Commission—to go into all the world and preach the Gospel—is, you cannot fulfill it without this. Jesus wasn't praying for Himself in the Lord's Prayer. He confessed sin, yet He didn't know any sin. This was a mandate for us. There is a realm, an unseen realm, that would manifest on this earth such that we would experience heaven. This was an invitation for us into the life of the supernatural.

We are living in the days of heaven on earth. We are called to bring that Kingdom here. Into our marriages, our jobs, our schools—as it is in heaven. Over our cities, our churches and our nation, we declare, "As it is in heaven."

Imagine living without knowledge of what is available to you spiritually. The devil wants nothing more for you. He wants you stuck in mediocrity, with spiritual gifts operating only at a low level, not seeing the glory of the Lord. There is so much more for you!

Years ago, a pastor friend of mine went overseas on a missions trip to the Middle East, and he had been preparing for it for some time. He had saved just enough money for the hotel. To help with food costs, he had prepackaged snacks that he could eat between meetings. He had some nuts, meats and chips he had brought from America. He was teaching a lot that week, and he saw God do powerful things.

The day he was supposed to check out of the hotel, he went downstairs to the lobby to catch his prearranged ride to the airport. When he was in the lobby, about to head out, one of the hotel staff approached him.

"Good morning, sir," said the host. "I want to make sure you enjoyed your stay here. How was your stay?"

"Great," said my pastor friend, still in a hurry to catch his ride.

"Are you sure, sir?" the hotel staffer asked again.

"Yes!" my friend said quickly. "Why do you keep asking?"

"We noticed you never joined us for any meals," said the staffer.

At that time, two double doors opened next to them off to the right. The place was filled with food—about eight buffet tables full.

"Sir, this food was included in your hotel stay, but you never came and ate with us."

"Wow, I didn't realize that," my friend replied.

This is the Kingdom. There are so many people in the "lobby" of faith, not experiencing all that was paid for. When Jesus died on the cross, grace made all things available to us. How much is ours? First Corinthians 3:21–23 says:

> So then, no more boasting about human leaders! All things are yours, whether Paul or Apollos or Cephas or the world or life or death or the present or the future—all are yours, and you are of Christ, and Christ is of God.

All things are yours and mine. How do we know how much the Father trusts us? By what He has entrusted to us. He has given us all things! We cannot continue to live beneath our privileges. Jesus died on the cross and then decided to give us everything. He equipped us to walk in authority on this earth. When Jesus said, "Tarry here and wait for the promise of the Father," He was having faith in the encounter they were about to experience (see Luke 24:49). This encounter would open up the earth to His glory.

Sadly, many Christians are unaware of what is open and available to them. They don't thirst for the "greater works" Jesus talks about in John 14:12 (NKJV): "Most assuredly, I say to you, he who believes in Me, the works that I do he will do also; and greater works than these he will do, because I go to My Father."

Accessing What's in Your Account

I have a close friend who was in a very traumatic car accident as a child. Truly horrific, and as a result, he lost a sibling. When he turned eighteen, he got a surprise. He would receive $250K from the car accident settlement. That's a quarter of a million dollars, and back then it was worth more than it is today! Can you imagine? That's a lot of money.

As you can imagine, my friend was over-the-top thrilled. It didn't matter what was happening the day he got that news. He had money coming into his account. If you were told that kind of news, it wouldn't matter if the bank came to repossess your car. You would be a different person with a different mindset. You would be aware of what had been given to you. I am sure you already can think of the bills you would pay and the people you would bless. When my friend heard the news, he didn't actually have the money. But he gained an understanding of what was about to be his. He became more aware.

As Christians, we are called to walk in the fullness of what we've been given. That starts with knowing what it is that's in our spiritual account. The enemy wants you to focus on your lack and focus on your issues. In essence, he wants to dislodge you from the awareness of what you have been given. Think about it—it's so much easier to focus on what we don't have than what we do have.

The gospel of John gives us an amazing declaration from Jesus: "When he had received the drink, Jesus said, 'It is finished.' With that, he bowed his head and gave up his spirit" (John 19:30). Those are the most powerful three words: *It is finished.* That means it was paid for in full. He wasn't just saying that His mission on earth was done; He was declaring that we have the money in our account now, so to speak.

The role of faith is to transfer what's in our account to what's in our possession. It is learning to make those faith withdrawals constantly. Again, "all things" are yours and mine. We've heard the phrase "Kingdom now and not yet," and to some degree I believe that is true. We cannot, however, allow the "not yet" to be a resting place for unbelief.

Paul's Secret in Ephesians

Paul the apostle wrote a letter to the church of Ephesus with great revelation and insight, which we now know as a book of the Bible. I believe that the book of Ephesians has within it keys to help us understand what we have been given. In fact, right from the very beginning we see some revelation keys:

> Paul, an apostle of Christ Jesus by the will of God, to God's holy people in Ephesus, the faithful in Christ Jesus: Grace and peace to you from God our Father and the Lord Jesus Christ.
>
> Ephesians 1:1–2

Did you catch it? Paul wrote, "to God's holy people in Ephesus," and then he called them "the faithful in Christ." This is a huge key. The same group of people are in two places! They are "in Ephesus," and also "in Christ." They are living on earth, but in the realms of heaven at the same time.

Paul would expound further in the next chapter and say,

> But because of his great love for us, God, who is rich in mercy, made us alive with Christ even when we were dead in transgressions—it is by grace you have been saved. And God raised us up with Christ and seated us with him in the heavenly realms in Christ Jesus.
>
> Ephesians 2:4–6

We are seated with Christ in heavenly places. We are seated on earth and in heaven. This is one of the greatest keys to honoring God's voice—an awareness that we live in two kingdoms at the same time. And you will reflect the kingdom you are most aware of.

When Paul opened the letter to the Ephesian church, there was so much revelation in his words. He continued in Ephesians 1:3, "Praise be to the God and Father of our Lord Jesus Christ, who has blessed us in the heavenly realms with every spiritual blessing in Christ." Not only are we living in the heavenly realms; at the same time we are also on earth. Paul reminds us that we are blessed with every spiritual blessing in the heavenly realms.

John Whittaker, from West Virginia, won 315 million dollars on a lottery ticket in 2002. Whittaker told *Time* magazine, "I wish that we had torn the ticket up." Later, both a daughter and a granddaughter would die of a drug overdose. Most lottery winners are usually bankrupt within three to five years.[2] God has entrusted us as His children with something far greater than any monetary value or winning lottery ticket. He gave us everything; we have it all now. He required that it would be accessed through Him, and what we do with it matters. Our response to the knowing matters. Our stewardship matters.

Prophecy Unlocks Miracles

Here is a key most people aren't aware that we have: prophecy. It unlocks miracles and even gives invitation for the miraculous. Years ago, I went to minister in a nearby country. This was an interesting trip because most of the area I was in was not Christian. When I left on the trip, the Lord spoke to me that in order to show the region and the people His power, He was going to do some mighty miracles in the church I was visiting. I believe God wants to invade the darkest places on the earth.

We saw so many miracles the weekend I was there. So many! One miracle that stood out to me was a mom who had dementia. She hadn't talked in several years! As I called all the sick forward for prayer, her kids escorted their mom up, who was older, and had her sit near the front. As I was praying for the sick, I glanced at her. She looked lifeless, just like a shell. We continued to pray, and one girl was healed of an ankle issue. She took her cast off and started running around the room. At this point I started praying in tongues, our heavenly prayer language. The applause of the crowd cheering over the ankle healing turned into the crowd praying in tongues. It was a powerful moment.

Then I walked up to this shell of a woman, and while I didn't know her story, I could see that she looked lost. I placed my hand on her head as I was praying in the Holy

Spirit, and then I started feeling a charge, like a fire running through my hand into her head. I continued to pray in tongues. Louder and louder it got, with the crowd also praying. Then the woman, to our surprise, jumped up out of the seat and started speaking in tongues!

This was the first time her family had heard any words from her in years. She quickly jumped up and grabbed my microphone from my hand. She told the church that for years the devil had had her tongue bound. She had been unable to speak, but could hear everything that was happening around her. That night, she said that as I laid my hands on her, "The devil loosed his hold from my tongue!"

This was truly an incredible miracle I will never forget. What happened from there was just as amazing. Let me first remind you that the Bible says in Revelation 19:10 (NKJV), "For the testimony of Jesus is the spirit of prophecy." I began to see something happen. Every time I shared that woman's story, faith would flood the room and people would get healed from dementia. The testimony of Jesus was a prophetic word for others to get set free!

When we testify, we release a prophetic word for others to step in and get free. These are truths that we must be aware of. Again, awareness of what we have been given will allow us to walk in all that God has, and we will hear His voice more sharply than ever before.

When a Drink Becomes a River

Jesus said we must thirst. And only in the Kingdom of God does a drink become a river! John 7:37–38 says this:

> On the last and greatest day of the festival, Jesus stood and said in a loud voice, "Let anyone who is thirsty come to me

and drink. Whoever believes in me, as Scripture has said, rivers of living water will flow from within them."

Jesus is saying that if we drink from Him, out of our innermost being will flow rivers—rivers of living water. We must drink. We must thirst, and this is the overflow God wants us to have. As we drink, it becomes a river. It is not a stagnant pool. It is not a stale body of water. It is a river, an ever-flowing river from heaven to earth.

Then the next verse says, "But this He spoke concerning the Spirit, whom those believing in Him would receive; for the Holy Spirit was not yet given, because Jesus was not yet glorified" (John 7:39 NKJV). Up until that time, the Spirit had not yet been given, because Jesus had not yet said, "It is finished." Jesus was speaking of what would happen in our lives after the Day of Pentecost.

The disciples didn't have the Bible. They later wrote the New Testament. So I believe the disciples had limited access at this point, because Jesus hadn't left yet. Now that Jesus has been glorified and is seated at the right hand of the Father, more than ever, we need to thirst and become aware of all we have been given. There are so many revelation treasures waiting to be discovered. And as we drink, a river will flow from within us.

I challenge you to empty yourself of any doctrine that restricts and hinders that awareness and that mighty flow from happening. There is an open heaven above you, and nothing is impossible for those who believe (see Luke 1:37). I pray today that you would begin to explore in faith all that revelation has revealed.

Prophetic Declaration and Prayer

Father, we thank You today for all You have made available to us. We thank You that we will be a generation that does greater works. We thank You that You have filled us with Your Holy Spirit and have given us everything we need in order to live this life.

I pray that by faith, we would access all You have made available to us. Thank You for the spirit of wisdom and revelation in the knowledge of You!

We declare that the greatest days are ahead, in Jesus' name! Amen.

Powerful Points about the Prophetic

- I believe the greatest hindrance to Christianity today is a lack of knowledge about what we've been given. We have been pressed by our lack of knowledge about what is available to us.

- In 1 Corinthians 2:12 (NKJV), it says, "Now we have received, not the spirit of the world, but the Spirit who is from God, that we might know the things that have been freely given to us by God." We have to know what He has given us, and value that knowledge.

- As important as the Great Commission—to go into all the world and preach the Gospel—is, we cannot fulfill it without understanding the mandate Jesus gave us to pray and live on earth as it is in heaven.

- There is an unseen realm that would manifest on this earth such that we would experience heaven. We are invited into the life of the supernatural, and we are called to bring that Kingdom here.

- As Christians, we are called to walk in the fullness of what we've been given. That starts with knowing what it is that's in our spiritual account.

- The enemy wants to dislodge us from that awareness of what we've been given. Think about it—it's so much easier to focus on what we don't have than on what we do have.

- The role of faith is to transfer what's in our account to what's in our possession. It is learning to make those faith withdrawals constantly.

- We've heard the phrase "Kingdom now and not yet," and to some degree it is true. We cannot, however, allow the "not yet" to be a resting place for unbelief.

- In Ephesians, the apostle Paul gave us some keys to help us understand what we've been given. For instance, he tells us we are blessed with every spiritual blessing in the heavenly realms.

- Paul also tells us we are seated with Christ in heavenly places. This is one of the greatest keys to honoring God's voice—an awareness that we live in two kingdoms at the same time.

- As you and I live out "on earth as it is in heaven," we will reflect the kingdom we are most aware of.

- Prophecy is a key most people aren't aware that we have. When we testify, we release a prophetic word for others to step in and get free. Prophecy unlocks miracles and even gives invitation for the miraculous.

- Jesus said if we drink from Him, out of our innermost being will flow rivers of living water (see John 7:37–38). We must drink. We must thirst, and this is the overflow God wants us to have.

- There is an open heaven above you and me, and nothing is impossible with those who believe (see Luke 1:37).

10

THE POWER OF WORDS

The Value of Our Speech

"Sticks and stones may break my bones, but words will never hurt me" is a phrase that originated in a book by Alexander Kinglake way back in 1844, but we still hear it today. When I was a kid, I would hear this phrase on the playground. At first, you are ingrained to think that words are not harmful. No matter what is said, the implication is that words cannot produce real harm. I believe, however, that words can destroy lives in a far worse way than material things can hurt us.

Years ago, I had a vision. I saw people living in nice houses, with great roofs protecting them from every storm. These homes were extra protected and seemed more reinforced than an average house. At the same time, I saw homes that were not fully built. Clearly, they gave no protection from any storm. Then I saw homes that were made of cardboard, and some that were even made of dirt.

I realized that depending on the house, your living situation would be drastically different from those around you. After seeing this, I asked the Lord what it meant. He said, *These homes were built by their own words. You are the prophet of your own life.*

From the very beginning, we see the power of words. Genesis 1:1–4 (NKJV) says,

> In the beginning God created the heavens and the earth. The earth was without form, and void; and darkness was on the face of the deep. And the Spirit of God was hovering over the face of the waters.
> Then God said, "Let there be light"; and there was light. And God saw the light, that it was good; and God divided the light from the darkness.

This world was formed by words. The same is true for our own world. Our words will determine the course of our lives. The Bible also tells us in Proverbs 18:21 (ESV), "Death and life are in the power of the tongue, and those who love it will eat its fruit."

Death and life are in the power of the tongue. We understand the power of life. We declare God's Word over our circumstances; we speak life when healings and miracles happen. We have to come to a place in God where we realize that words can create life. Yet Scripture tells us that death is also in our tongue. As a believer, you have power and authority, and the devil knows that. We have to use our words to speak life and not death.

As a pastor, I will tell you that the person who says "I am sick" and the person who says "I am healed" are both right.

The person who says "I can't afford it" and the person who says "I am blessed beyond measure" are also both right. They are right because of their own words.

One day, I was talking to a woman who had just come out of a bad relationship. She said in frustration, "All men are dogs!" She followed that by, "I've always believed that." Guess who is still single?

I made it clear to this woman that although it isn't a weird hocus-pocus game, when we make declarations like that, the devil will use those words. Our confession matters. We must not confuse our confession. The Bible is clear that we need to flee idle talk, and that by our words we will be acquitted and condemned (see 2 Timothy 2:16; Matthew 12:37). We have to learn to speak God's Word and not allow our words to be used as a tool of the devil.

The same goes for ministers of the Gospel. Anytime I see a man of God tearing down other ministers or using his gift to tear people down, I know it is only a matter of time before judgment comes. We cannot be ministers who are using our mouths to declare the devil's plan. Our words have power. Even "joking" isn't a good reason to trash men of God or talk down to the people of God. We must rise to a higher standard of living.

We read in 2 Corinthians 4:13 (NKJV), "And since we have the same spirit of faith, according to what is written, 'I believed and therefore I spoke,' we also believe and therefore speak." This Scripture is clear—we believe, then we speak what we believe. I do not want to use my words as a tool for hell.

On many occasions, people will come into my office in financial despair, with their marriage on the verge of breaking up or just struggling in their own lives. So many times, the Lord will simply instruct me to tell them to change their words. That's it. Start confessing the Word every day. Declare life every day. Declare you are blessed every day. You know what will happen? God will manifest His Word as we speak it!

Walk in It

The Bible says in Job 22:28 (NKJV), "You will also declare a thing, and it will be established for you; so light will shine on your ways." I am not talking about "name it and claim it," or some 1980s abused theology. I am telling you that as you declare God's Word only, you will see heaven flood in. By declaring what the Word says, you will walk in exactly what you believe.

Raising children today is not an easy task. There's no doubt that this is one of the hardest times in history to navigate being a parent. Schools seem to have a demonic agenda, and there's the Internet and worldly influences we have to shield our kids from, all while leading them in the way they should go in faith. It is not easy apart from the Holy Spirit. Parents have to rely on the Holy Spirit.

In chapter 1, I shared my children's daily declaration. It began one day as I sent my son off to school. I was praying for him, as I always prayed before he got out of the car. As I was driving home, I thought, *I want him to declare, not just me!* I wanted my son to walk into school with confidence, his head held high, knowing the Word of the Lord over his life. So I began to write a declaration that he could say every day. And, friend, I mean *every day*. We started when he was four, and now all our kids declare it daily. We even have it posted in their bedrooms. Here it is again:

> *I am a leader, not a follower,*
> *I am the head and not the tail,*
> *I am above and not beneath,*

I am a lender, not the borrower,
I am blessed and highly favored,
And I'm going to change this world!

It fires me up just writing that. Can you imagine declaring this over your life every day, and having your kids declare it over their lives, too? You know what will start happening? Your children will go through their day and remember it. When they are tempted to be the tail, they will be the head. When they are being peer-pressured into following, they will lead instead. When you declare every day that you are a leader and not a follower, you will walk in not only what you have been saying, but in what God says in His Word.

Our Speech Can Change Cities

I believe that not only does the Lord want to change our lives and the lives of others by our speech, but that cities and regions can also be shaken as we declare God's Word. Isaiah 61 is a powerful chapter. It is the Scripture Jesus read aloud in the synagogue in Luke 4, and I believe it contains revelation about our speech:

> The Spirit of the Lord GOD is upon Me, because the LORD has anointed Me to preach good tidings to the poor; He has sent Me to heal the brokenhearted, to proclaim liberty to the captives, and the opening of the prison to those who are bound; to proclaim the acceptable year of the LORD, and the day of vengeance of our God.
>
> Isaiah 61:1–2 NKJV

In this Scripture, we see fruit. We see God healing the brokenhearted. We see liberty and freedom for the captives. We see prisons opening for those who are bound. This would be considered amazing fruit in any life. Notice that all the fruit comes by speech! Preach, proclaim and declare is how it all happened. When we think of God moving powerfully, we may think of prayer alone, or we may think of hard work, but God shows us in this Scripture that it is by our words that we will see these things happen! Preaching, proclaiming and declaring!

Then something else happens as a result in verse 4 (NKJV) of this same passage: "And they shall rebuild the old ruins, they shall raise up the former desolations, and they shall re-pair the ruined cities, the desolations of many generations." Now we see another level taking place. We see cities restored. We see nations changed. We see God restore and raise up in this verse. But who are "they" who do this rebuilding? When the Scripture says "they," whom is it referring to? "They" are the people who were spoken to in the first verses. Through speech—the preaching, proclaiming and declaring—we see a group of people set free. We see a group of people get delivered, and then *they* go out restoring cities and regions. There is clear value placed here on our words. Imagine that as we preach and declare, cities in turn will be transformed!

When I became born again, I was completely transformed. I didn't need a pep talk to share my faith; I didn't need anyone encouraging me to speak up. When I was touched by God, my mouth opened and I began to preach, proclaim and declare. When you and I speak, when we understand the value of our words, we will see the fruit of our proclamation.

On the other hand, when we don't speak, people can remain enslaved. The Bible shows us this also, in Isaiah 42:21–23 (NKJV):

The LORD is well pleased for His righteousness' sake; He will exalt the law and make it honorable. But this is a people

151

robbed and plundered; all of them are snared in holes, and they are hidden in prison houses; they are for prey, and no one delivers; for plunder, and no one says, "Restore!" Who among you will give ear to this? Who will listen and hear for the time to come?

Here, we see the result of not speaking. We see a warning about a people who are robbed, plundered, trapped and in prison, and the Lord says that no one will say "Restore!" There is a danger if we do not open our mouths and preach, proclaim and declare.

Faith, Words and Belief

Let's look at the connection between faith and our words. I believe there is revelation God wants us to understand with this powerful connection. Let's look at some Scriptures about this that we find in the Gospels.

Our words, backed by faith, can produce the Kingdom of God in our lives. In Mark 9:23 (NKJV), Jesus says, "If you can believe, all things are possible to him who believes." Immediately, we realize belief is the most powerful force in our lives. Belief in Jesus. Belief in His Word.

How does that belief get activated? Look what Jesus says in Matthew 17:14–20 (NKJV):

And when they had come to the multitude, a man came to Him, kneeling down to Him and saying, "Lord, have mercy on my son, for he is an epileptic and suffers severely; for he often falls into the fire and often into the water. So I brought him to Your disciples, but they could not cure him."

Then Jesus answered and said, "O faithless and perverse generation, how long shall I be with you? How long shall I bear with you? Bring him here to Me." And Jesus rebuked the demon, and it came out of him; and the child was cured from that very hour.

Then the disciples came to Jesus privately and said, "Why could we not cast it out?"

So Jesus said to them, "Because of your unbelief; for assuredly, I say to you, if you have faith as a mustard seed, you will say to this mountain, 'Move from here to there,' and it will move; and nothing will be impossible for you."

Faith and speech. Again, Jesus gives us a key to faith activation, and it is our speech. What Jesus is saying is that nothing is impossible if you say what you believe. All things are possible with those who believe—and who speak it!

Jesus even likens our faith to a small mustard seed, and He says if we are willing to speak, mountains will be removed. Further highlighting, this means it's not only the size of our faith, but the words that accompany it. We cannot say we have a belief and not be willing to speak it. When we continually condition ourselves to speak empty words, or words we do not believe, we hinder the activation of our faith. Our faith is not fully expressed until we believe and speak God's Word.

In everyday life, we have opportunities to speak life. I was with a minister and his family at a park. As everyone was playing, his child fell and scraped her knee. Of course, the young girl was hurt and probably a bit embarrassed. I watched as the dad went over and asked if she was okay. The mom followed. Clearly hurt, the child couldn't really get up at first. After a few minutes, however, she was okay again and went back to playing.

I asked the dad why he didn't pray for his daughter. Why didn't he take authority over that accident and curse it? (By which I mean verbally breaking off any attack from the devil.)

My questions really encouraged him to begin to take authority around his home and start declaring the Word of God.

We all have opportunities in our day-to-day lives to speak life. We have to remember that it's not real faith unless it's spoken out!

This is not a theory. It is a spiritual law. Jesus never did anything without first speaking it. Then what Jesus said turned into what Jesus saw. And today, we find ourselves doing everything without speaking. Everything we believe, we need to speak, and then God manifests. There is so much more God wants to give you in life if you will just release your faith in words. Everything I have received in my life, I have received through declaring and believing.

What Do You Believe?

We use the word *believe* a lot. Alone, it is incomplete. Our belief needs to be put into some words. There are so many people today waiting for miracles that God is waiting for them to declare. Mountains are waiting to be moved by us!

In Mark 11:12–14, Jesus was walking by a fig tree. It appeared to be alive, but it wasn't bearing fruit. As He walked by, He cursed it. This was unusual for the disciples to witness; they hadn't quite seen that side of Jesus. They always heard life come forth, and now He had cursed something. The next morning as they were walking, they asked Him about it:

> Now in the morning, as they passed by, they saw the fig tree dried up from the roots. And Peter, remembering, said to Him, "Rabbi, look! The fig tree which You cursed has withered away."
> So Jesus answered and said to them, "Have faith in God. For assuredly, I say to you, whoever says to this mountain, 'Be

removed and be cast into the sea,' and does not doubt in his heart, but believes that those things he says will be done, he will have whatever he says. Therefore I say to you, whatever things you ask when you pray, believe that you receive them, and you will have them."

Mark 11:20–24 NKJV

Again, we need to believe that those things we say will be done. Jesus was using this fig tree to explain that we must speak the words that we believe. We must have the same faith God has. "Have faith in God" has also been translated as "Have the God kind of faith."[1]

Ephesians 5:1 (NKJV) says, "Therefore be imitators of God as dear children." If we truly are called to imitate Him, then that means in speech as well as in action. The Bible would not have asked us to imitate God if this was not possible. And as we examine the life of Jesus, we see Him speaking to many things, including wind, seas, demons, fig trees, dead people . . . Guess what—they all obeyed!

Keys of the Kingdom

Matthew 16:19 (NKJV) says, "And I will give you the keys of the kingdom of heaven, and whatever you bind on earth will be bound in heaven, and whatever you loose on earth will be loosed in heaven." We see in this verse an established Kingdom. You are doing something with your speech that is already established in heaven.

When you or I say "I am healed," that is because it was already done. When we declare "I am blessed," that is because it has already been established. We are not merely creating scenarios in our flesh that we beg for by our words. We are declaring with our mouths what we believe—what has already been established. So when we speak and pray, it is commanding things that God has already established. Our belief and our words bring heaven to earth.

Psalm 119:89 (NKJV) says, "Forever, O LORD, Your word is settled in heaven." When we speak His Word, we are not "hoping" it is settled. It is already settled in heaven.

It is your job and mine to establish His Word on the earth. God has already produced it; now we are called to produce it on the earth, bind it on the earth and settle it on the earth.

• Whose Word Will You Establish?

In Psalm 89:34 the Lord says, "I will not violate my covenant or alter what my lips have uttered." God will never change anything He has said. His Word is forever settled and established. Now we must decide what we will choose to speak. Whose kingdom will you and I be advancing? If it is God's Kingdom, then we must speak God's words.

The power of binding and loosing relies on the worth in our words. We must program ourselves to speak with the authority we have been given. Spoken words will prepare you and me for success or defeat. Words are spiritual containers that carry either faith or fear, and will produce after their own kind.

Today, decide that you will use your words for life. Resolve that from this day forward, you will begin to bind and loose, and that you will restore God's Kingdom on this earth with your speech. This is truly the most powerful tool that we have as believers, one that rarely is fully understood.

Prophetic Declaration and Prayer

Father, I thank You that You have placed Your authority within us, and that You have called us to be co-heirs with Christ. I thank You today that we now understand the power of our words.

I pray that from this day forward, we will go out and declare Your Word, what You have already established, and that we will declare it and settle it on this earth!

We vow to speak only that which we know comes from You. In a day when so many empty words are being thrown around, we choose life, we choose heaven. We choose You! In the mighty name of Jesus, Amen.

Powerful Points about the Prophetic

- Years ago, when I had a vision of people living in houses of every sort, from nice, sturdy homes to cardboard and dirt hovels, the Lord explained it to me this way: *These homes were built by their own words. You are the prophet of your own life.*

- This world was formed by words (see Genesis 1). The same is true for our own world. Our words will determine the course of our lives. That's why our speech is so valuable.

- "Death and life are in the power of the tongue," Proverbs 18:21 (NKJV) tells us. As believers we have power and authority, and the devil knows that. We have to use our words to speak life and not death.

- By declaring what the Word says, you will walk in exactly what you believe. When you declare every day that you are a leader and not a follower (and teach your children to do the same), you will walk in not only what you have been saying, but in what God says in His Word.

- Not only does the Lord want to change our lives and the lives of others by our speech, but cities and regions can also be shaken as we declare God's Word.

- Notice that all fruit comes by speech. When we think of God moving powerfully, we may think of prayer alone, or we may think of hard work, but God shows us in Isaiah 61:1–2 that it is by our words that we see things happen like people being set free—by our preaching, proclaiming and declaring!

- When you and I speak, we will see the fruit of our proclamation. On the other hand, when we don't speak, people might remain enslaved. There is a danger if we do not open our mouths and preach, proclaim and declare.

- Our words, backed by faith, can produce the Kingdom of God in our lives. In Mark 9:23 (NKJV), Jesus says, "If you can believe, all things are possible to him who believes." Belief is the most powerful force in our lives.

- We cannot say we have a belief and not be willing to speak it. When we continually condition ourselves to speak empty words, or words we do not believe, we hinder the activation of our faith. Our faith is not fully expressed unless we are believing and speaking God's Word.

- Ephesians 5:1 (NKJV) says, "Therefore be imitators of God as dear children." If we truly are called to imitate Him, then that means in speech as well as in action. We see Jesus speaking to many things, including wind, seas, demons, fig trees, dead people . . . and they all obeyed!

- It is our job to establish God's Word on the earth. He has already produced it; now we are called to produce it on the earth, bind it on the earth and settle it on the earth (see Matthew 16:19; Psalm 119:89).

- Words are spiritual containers that carry either faith or fear, and will produce after their own kind. Our speech is truly the most powerful tool that we have as believers, and one that rarely is fully understood.

11

LIVING TO GIVE

The Value of Generosity

Generosity. The prophetic value of generosity is unquestionably one of the greatest keys to unlocking and hearing God's voice. How we view God and how we view generosity will determine what we believe is possible and how generous we will be.

I will let you in on a secret. As a pastor, I do not look weekly at who tithes. Of course, we monitor the cash flow, the church budgets and the offerings. But as far as individual giving goes, I do not see that until the end of the year. Why? Mainly because it is not the focus for me. I trust that God provides, and I realize He is the source. Also, I never want any family treated differently based on how much or how little they give.

But I absolutely will tell you that although I do not look weekly at who is giving what amount, I can tell who is giving by what their lives look like. With people who struggle in the area of giving, you can see the unbelief in other areas of their lives. But people who trust God in the area of giving are generous, they hear from God, and it spills over into every other area.

Paul called it "giving and receiving" throughout the New Testament. You cannot choose one or the other; they come together. If we are going to learn how to hear from God, which is receiving, then we must learn to give. We must pass the test of treasure if we are to excel in the gifts we have been given to their fullest.

The Spirit of Withholding

When I was born again, I was amazed as I went to various churches and saw something I couldn't even fathom. The churches that didn't allow the Holy Spirit to move freely also didn't believe in or experience giving, and they didn't look to the Father as a generous God.

The dead-religion mindset (otherwise known as a spirit of religion) you see in that kind of church is a withholding spirit not just in faith, but in money. Proverbs 11:24–25 (NKJV) tells us:

> There is one who scatters, yet increases more; and there is one who withholds more than is right, but it leads to poverty. The generous soul will be made rich, and he who waters will also be watered himself.

We see in this passage one person who scatters, and one person who increases more. One person is pouring out, and God is pouring in. The other person is holding back what is right, and it leads to poverty. In our lives, this is so true. Withholding leads to poverty, and a poverty spirit. When we are generous, and as we scatter, we will increase continuously.

What we do in the area of giving sets a constant pattern of increasing or withholding in our lives.

Jesus said in Matthew 10:8 (NKJV), "Freely you have received, freely give." We are called to walk in the principles of God's generosity; we are called to live a life of giving. Recently, I posted a video on Instagram in which I reflected on leaving Connecticut and some of the struggles we had, and how God broke through for us that year. It was a vulnerable post in which I wanted to give God the glory. And although people wrote to me and said they cried, rejoiced and were so blessed by the post, someone got on and commented, "Prosperity Preacher Alert."

I was taken aback. What was even more amazing to me is that this was the third time in a week someone tried to attack me and say that kind of thing about me. I took it as a compliment that somehow in my life, God has blessed us to a place where there's no other option but for my critics to say that I am blessed. That's incredible!

What I replied to the one gentleman was, "Can you do me a favor please and believe prosperity also? We feed up to a hundred homeless a day and take care of orphans and widows, and we could use the help. Thanks." I realized that right in front of my eyes, God has fulfilled His Word enough to cause people to get angry because we are blessed.

The Word Works

When I got saved, I really got saved. I remember reading the Bible and longing to see signs and wonders. I wanted visitations from God. I wanted to see visions and hear God's voice clearly. As I read the Word, I began to see the nature of our Father. And I began to think Kingdom. Everything was Kingdom.

Financially, I couldn't have cared less about my life. All I wanted was to expand God's Kingdom. I grew up in a very poor neighborhood in Connecticut. I never had money for lunch at school, and my mom and I relied on food stamps or government assistance. I dropped out of high school. I can promise you that I was not a person anyone would think God could use. Having a child at sixteen only made it more difficult. You wouldn't have called me into the ministry. I didn't fit people's mold.

As I grew closer to God, money became Kingdom to me. I worked to make sure I could give and could expand the reach of the Gospel. And I realized a secret: When I gave radically to God, He would give it right back. It was truly a place where I couldn't outgive God.

When I started my first churches, I sometimes used my whole paycheck to feed the homeless, just to sow into the Kingdom. Sowing was, and still is, my top desire. Money to me is a Kingdom resource, and God is looking for those who will allow Him to pass money through them to expand the Kingdom.

Two Masters

In Matthew 6:19–24 (NKJV), Jesus explains the power of generosity:

> Do not lay up for yourselves treasures on earth, where moth and rust destroy and where thieves break in and steal; but lay up for yourselves treasures in heaven, where neither moth nor rust destroys and where thieves do not break in and steal. For where your treasure is, there your heart will be also.
> The lamp of the body is the eye. If therefore your eye is good, your whole body will be full of light. But if your eye is bad, your whole body will be full of darkness. If therefore the light that is in you is darkness, how great is that darkness!

No one can serve two masters; for either he will hate the one and love the other, or else he will be loyal to the one and despise the other. You cannot serve God and mammon.

We see two powerful truths here. First, we are told to store up our treasures in heaven. We all have treasures; we all have a choice about where we want to place our treasures. Jesus warns us not to store up our treasures on earth, where they can be stolen or perish. He encourages us to sow into the Kingdom and store up our treasures in heaven, where they will never perish. The reward is eternal.

In Acts 10:4 (NKJV), when Cornelius inquired of the Lord, an angel told him, "Your prayers and your alms have come up for a memorial before God." God was telling Cornelius that his offerings and prayers had built a memorial in heaven! Can you imagine if every prayer you ever prayed, and everything you ever gave financially, became a memorial before God? I think it will. I believe this is a part of storing up "treasures in heaven."

When my wife and I have a need, we pray, and the first thing we ask ourselves is, *What have we planted? Have we stored up treasures in heaven?* Because that's the place of the blessing of the Lord, the place from which all else flows.

The second powerful truth in Matthew 6 is about serving two masters. Jesus said, "No one can serve two masters; for either he will hate the one and love the other, or else he will be loyal to the one and despise the other. You cannot serve God and mammon" (verse 24 NKJV). Money is a horrible master. Jesus is the perfect Savior.

Jesus said if we are not careful, we will love one master and despise the other. When people love money, they despise teaching on giving. They "hate" anything to do with prosperity or blessing. This shows a love for the god of mammon.

The principle here can be found in one question: Who or what is your source? It is easy when we work all week to think that our source is our job, or whoever pays us. Do not be confused—our source is Jesus. Heaven is the source of all we do, and we have to remember continually to stay locked into the source of all our supply. You will be tempted at times to make the wrong choice about whom you see as your source. Remember, it is not people or money; it is always Jesus.

This is a huge spiritual test for most people. I am always amused when someone comes into the church or into my office and wants to debate tithing. "Is tithing in the New Testament?" they ask. "Do I have to give 10 percent?" They all want to try to convince me that tithing is Old Testament.

The truth is, tithing is for today. The only difference is, it's now 100 percent. The tithe, 10 percent, is just a basic starting gauge for us as Christians. The real standard is 100 percent. Everything we have is God's, and at any moment He can require you or me to give it all away. That's the real answer. The moment you are arguing or debating over a tithe, you've already fallen in love with the god of mammon.

There is a whole world of Kingdom expansion that many believers will not see. There is a place of giving and generosity that we can miss out on because we despise truth. I know people who are so hung up over someone owing them money that it has robbed them of their blessing. Because of choosing to live by the wrong principle, they now look at a human being as their source or provider.

I have lost track of how many times I have heard God say to me, *Forgive and move on; I will repay you.* Nothing is worth more than the peace of God on this earth. And so many Christians get stuck because they are expecting someone else to give them what the Father wanted to give them.

⬤ Seed to the Sower

In 2 Corinthians 9:6–10 (NKJV), Paul lays out some powerful keys about sowing and reaping:

> But this I say: He who sows sparingly will also reap sparingly, and he who sows bountifully will also reap bountifully. So let each one give as he purposes in his heart, not grudgingly or of necessity; for God loves a cheerful giver. And God is able to make all grace abound toward you, that you, always having all sufficiency in all things, may have an abundance for every good work. As it is written:
> "He has dispersed abroad, He has given to the poor; His righteousness endures forever."
> Now may He who supplies seed to the sower, and bread for food, supply and multiply the seed you have sown and increase the fruits of your righteousness.

You are a spiritual farmer, whether you realize it or not. We are always sowing; we are always harvesting. The truth is that many people don't realize it, and many aren't happy with what they are reaping. If you do not like what you are reaping, you have to consider what you are sowing.

Here are four takeaways from this passage:

1. He who sows sparingly reaps sparingly. We must continually purpose in our hearts to live generously. Every prophetic word you have received has attached to it the finances and provisions needed so that it can come to pass. We have to believe that God can do anything. And as we sow, we will reap.

2. God wants us to have an abundance for "every good work." God wants to provide for you and your ministry and everything you put your hand to for the

Kingdom. God's people should never be without. It is the Father's desire that we have an abundance for everything we are called to do.

3. God gives seed to the sower. Years ago, I read this and believed I needed more seed before I sowed. It's not about the seed; more seed comes after we sow what we have. God gives to the sower. Are you a sower? The only way we get more seed is to sow. That's the only way. We must be sowers first, and then watch more seed come.

4. God's language is "supply and multiply." This is the language of the Kingdom, that our lives fixated on heaven will be multiplied. God wants to multiply everything in our lives.

Seed and the Kingdom

Everything is in seed form. Our lives are a seed. God works through seed. We see it in Genesis 8:22 (NKJV): "While the earth remains, seedtime and harvest, cold and heat, winter and summer, and day and night shall not cease."

Some things will never change while the earth remains. God tells us that day and night will never cease. He also says seedtime and harvest won't change. God has established this life—that by planting seeds, we will see fruit that will never cease. He has orchestrated a time of planting and a time of harvesting. A time of giving and a time of receiving. Galatians 6:7–10 (NKJV) tells us this:

Do not be deceived, God is not mocked; for whatever a man sows, that he will also reap. For he who sows to his flesh will of the flesh reap corruption, but he who sows to the Spirit will of the Spirit reap everlasting life. And let us not grow weary while doing good, for in due season we shall reap if we do not lose heart. Therefore, as we have opportunity, let us do good to all, especially to those who are of the household of faith.

You are always sowing. Some people today sow discord; some sow life. Do not be deceived. God is not mocked. Essentially, what this is saying is that it's a mockery to think you will sow a seed and will not reap! If you sow, it will grow.

Also, Paul tells us not to grow weary in well doing, because in due season we will reap. I am telling you that we are required to sow. God will bring increase in due season. Just like a tree, in season you will bear fruit. God has promised you that reaping and sowing will never leave this earth. We must continue declaring life and sowing the Word of God and all that we have.

● Stay Planted by the River

I have always loved palm trees, always. When I was living in Connecticut, I purchased a palm tree and had it shipped. (Who would have thought there was a palm tree tax in that state?) I was told the palm tree would survive in our climate. Well, one year in, and after three snowstorms, the palm tree died. The soil became too cold for the tree.

Fast-forward to when I moved to Florida. Now I have planted fruit trees. In Clearwater, Florida, the soil is surrounded by water, and it is a perfect soil for producing crops. Everything seems to thrive near the water sources.

Psalm 1:1–3 (NKJV) tells us about the blessed life. David describes what the characteristics are of someone who is blessed:

Blessed is the man who walks not in the counsel of the ungodly, nor stands in the path of sinners, nor sits in the seat of the scornful; but his delight is in the law of the LORD, and in His law he meditates day and night. He shall be like a tree planted by the rivers of water, that brings forth its fruit in its season, whose leaf also shall not wither; and whatever he does shall prosper.

When you are blessed, whatever you do will prosper!

First of all, someone who is blessed avoids sitting with the scornful. We should be surrounding ourselves with other godly people who love the Word of God and devour it. And David says we are planted by the river, and whatever we do will prosper. When we stay plugged into the Holy Spirit (the River), we are guaranteed to prosper in whatever we do. Decide today that you will flourish in every season and stay planted by the river.

We are called to live generously. I can promise you, the way we view God and biblical generosity will determine the positioning of our hearts to hear from Him. His voice is the fruit of being planted by the river. His voice is the fruit of sowing radically. Your life is a seed, and every day you have to continue to sow seeds of faith and righteousness.

I believe that from this moment on, you will begin to sow radically and reap radically. It is time to live to give. You and I must recognize that everything is in seed form, and that our supply comes from Jesus. And as we sow, He guarantees that we will reap a harvest.

God Is a Rewarder

The final key about generosity that I want you to know today is that God is a rewarder. God has a reward system in heaven, and as we tap into it, we will be blessed by bringing honor to Him. Hebrews 11:6 (NKJV) tells us, "Without faith it is impossible to please Him, for he who comes to God must believe that He is, and that He is a rewarder of those who diligently seek Him."

God is a rewarder, and as we have already talked about, He will reward us for our financial giving and for sowing seed. Now, we also realize that He is a rewarder of those who seek Him! God will pour out a greater measure of power and blessing on those who seek Him.

This is the hour to seek the Lord. This book is a clarion call for believers to get away in prayer and begin to hear God like never before. We are going to hear God's voice with clarity, and He will begin to unlock the mysteries of heaven in your life and mine in the days ahead.

Get ready for an explosion to take place as we seek the Lord! Get ready for promises to be fulfilled this year in your life, for dreams to come to pass, and for prophetic words to come to pass. This is the time for supernatural supply to be released in your life. I am excited for the days ahead!

Prophetic Declaration and Prayer

Father, we thank You for Your radical generosity, and for helping us to be like You in it. I pray that today, each of us will know the nature of Your Kingdom and know that You are the God who rewards.

You are the God who desires to supply and multiply. As we sow today, let the seeds of our lives spring forth and produce fruit for the Kingdom!

I thank You that we will begin to hear Your voice and sow seed (prophetic words) on this earth, in Jesus' name! Amen.

Powerful Points about the Prophetic

- Generosity is one of the greatest prophetic keys to unlocking and hearing God's voice. How we view God and how we view generosity will determine what we believe is possible and how generous we will be.
- There is such great value in generosity. People who trust God in the area of giving are generous, they hear from God, and it spills over into every other area.
- If we are going to learn how to hear from God, which is receiving, then we must learn to give. We must pass the test of treasure if we are to excel in the gifts we have been given to their fullest.
- Withholding leads to a poverty spirit. When we are generous, and as we scatter, we will increase continuously. What we do in the area of giving sets a constant pattern of increasing or withholding in our lives.
- Money to me is a Kingdom resource, and God is looking for those who will allow Him to pass money through them to expand the Kingdom.
- Can you imagine if every prayer you ever prayed, and everything you ever gave financially, became a memorial before God? I think it will. I believe this is a part of storing up "treasures in heaven" (see Matthew 6:19–24; Acts 10:4).
- Money is a horrible master. Jesus is the perfect Savior. The principle here can be found in one question: Who or what is your source?
- You are a spiritual farmer, whether you realize it or not. We are always sowing; we are always harvesting. . . . If you do not like what you are reaping, you have to consider what you are sowing.

- In 2 Corinthians 9:6–10, Paul lays out some powerful keys about sowing and reaping. Four important takeaways from this passage are that he who sows sparingly reaps sparingly, that God wants us to have an abundance for "every good work," that God gives seed to the sower and that God's language is "supply and multiply."

- We are required to sow. God will bring increase in due season. Just like a tree, in season you and I will bear fruit.

- When we stay plugged into the Holy Spirit (the River), we are guaranteed to prosper in whatever we do (see Psalm 1:1–3).

- The way we view God and biblical generosity will determine the positioning of our hearts to hear from Him. His voice is the fruit of being planted by the river. His voice is the fruit of sowing radically.

- You and I must recognize that everything is in seed form, and that our supply comes from Jesus. And as we sow, He guarantees we will reap a harvest.

- God is a rewarder. God has a reward system in heaven, and as we tap into it, we will be blessed by bringing honor to Him (see Hebrews 11:6).

- God is also a rewarder of those who seek Him! God will pour out a greater measure of power and blessing on those who seek Him. This is the hour to seek the Lord.

12

POSITIONING FOR THE PROPHETIC

Preparing for Your Suddenly

You *will* see the voice of the Lord increased in your life! I believe that the 10 prophetic values we talked about in these pages are inspired by God and have been strategically given to us for this season. Let's look at them one more time:

1. The value of integrity
2. The value of priority
3. The value of perseverance
4. The value of emotional health
5. The value of relationships
6. The value of loving the written Word of God
7. The value of endless hope
8. The value of knowing what we've been given

9. The value of our speech

10. The value of generosity

As I said at the start, when we put these 10 values into practice, they will help us listen to and glorify God's voice, the way we must in this day we are living in.

When it comes to God's promises, we have to realize that every single promise He has given us is conditional. Our ability to receive each promise comes down to what you and I are willing to do to see it come to pass. Nothing just "happens." Fulfilled promises are a result of prayer, faith and positioning. How we are positioned will determine our harvest!

The Bible is very clear on the conditions for receiving the promises of God. In 2 Chronicles 7:14 (NKJV) the Lord says, "If My people who are called by My name will humble themselves, and pray and seek My face, and turn from their wicked ways, then I will hear from heaven, and will forgive their sin and heal their land." In this passage, we see God declaring something amazing to His people—that He is going to heal their land! We all want our land to be healed. We all want our lives transformed. But most people do not want to "turn from their wicked ways" so their land can be healed.

I often think about healing. In Exodus 15:26 it says,

If you listen carefully to the LORD your God and do what is right in his eyes, if you pay attention to his commands and keep all his decrees, I will not bring on you any of the diseases I brought on the Egyptians, for I am the LORD, who heals you.

Of course, He is our healer. But it is easy to walk away quoting the part of this verse that says "I am the LORD, who heals you" and forget that He asks us to "listen carefully" and "pay attention to his commands" and "keep all his decrees." Standing on the Word of God and obeying His instructions about the way we should live will position us for hearing His voice.

Years of Positioning

People ask me all the time, "How did you learn to hear God's voice?"

I almost laugh in response because it's a good question. It really is something we must learn. We understand that God is always speaking, and as we learned already in this book, like Samuel, we can learn to hear God's voice when we are positioned in His presence. Over time, we learn to discern when what we hear is from God and when it is not. When we position ourselves like Samuel, we can walk away in confidence, knowing what the Lord is speaking.

I was invited to a revival conference to speak. I also decided to attend a morning session because I had heard a lot about a particular minister who was going to attend. I was seeing many miracles and salvations taking place on the streets and in my first church. Yet I was only about 23 years old at the time and had so much more to experience. I was very open to the prophetic and wanted to learn more. I will never forget how at the end of the session, this prophet stood up and said, "We are about to go to heaven."

I was intrigued! The prophet told all of us that we couldn't pray out loud and that we needed to be still. He was about to ask the Lord to take us up and show us visions or words if God wanted to. Let me clarify that I do not believe we can "go to heaven" at will, but I do believe as our spirit wills and as we position ourselves, God will speak to and visit us in many ways.

So this prophet began to pray, and immediately I felt the Lord's presence so strongly. A few moments later, he prayed, "Holy Spirit, come." Then he said, "Father, take us up. Show us the realms of Your Kingdom!"

Friend, I was overwhelmed. Immediately I saw a brook streaming down a mountainside, with rocks in it. It was a beautiful scene, the first vision I had ever had. I was blown away. *Does God speak in visions?* I wondered. *Can we experience this all the time?* I was going to find out.

I turned to my friend and said, "This moment will change our lives forever." To me, that was a moment of revelation, knowing that the Father wants to speak to us and that it is all about positioning. I went home, gathered our leaders and friends together, and made a charge. From that day on, we would gather together every day for two years to worship and meditate, and to begin learning how to hear God's voice!

You read that right—two years. Christmas, weekends, holidays, it didn't matter. About fifteen of us would meet every morning just to learn how to hear and experience God's voice, just as we had experienced it in that conference meeting. We were silent and still at first, listening to God, but we would later add music to our time together.

To start, I gave everyone a piece of paper and asked them to write down anything God showed them. We set some ground rules, too: "If something lines up with the Word of God, write it down. Or even if you think it's neutral, write it down." Over time, we put on file two years of images, words and pictures that we believed the Lord had shown us.

This was about positioning. I wasn't concerned with false words; I was concerned about learning how to hear God's voice with clarity. Too often, we don't create a safe space to learn to hear God, and I wanted to create a non-threatening environment where we could hear Him.

In the beginning, there were a lot of blank sheets of paper. By the end of two years, however, we were writing down names, dates, colors of clothing, and specific words, and then we would watch the words come to pass. Literally hundreds of stories of miracles resulted in our city, in our hometowns, even some nationally.

The best part about filing away the things we were shown is that we were able to go back and realize what was from God and, equally as important, what was not. We learned to hear with clarity. To this day, I know how to hear God clearly, and it all goes back to those two years of commitment and obedience to positioning ourselves to hear the Lord. Two years of being still.

Today, I will wake up and go to the ocean and pray. The coastline looks the same as it did over twenty years ago. I position myself to hear God's voice, and He meets me there. I can only tell you, positioning is everything.

God of the Suddenly

I feel the Lord speaking to me right now. I believe as we make room for Him, He will make room for us. I am telling you today, increase your time with Jesus. Make room just to be. And then watch the "suddenlies" happen in your life. A greater anointing is coming upon you. I see oil coming from heaven upon your head.

This will be a year of miracles. Instantaneous, overnight miracles. As you lean into the Kingdom and position yourself, suddenlies will happen! Prayers you no longer pray will be answered. Resurrected dreams of old, new purposes in God, and anointing belong to you.

I want to share a story from the book of Samuel. I believe this is a prophetic story on the topic of "suddenlies." In 1 Samuel 9:3–4 (NKJV), we read this story about Saul:

> Now the donkeys of Kish, Saul's father, were lost. And Kish said to his son Saul, "Please take one of the servants with you, and arise, go and look for the donkeys." So he passed through the mountains of Ephraim and through the land of Shalisha, but they did not find them. Then they passed through the land of Shaalim, and they were not there. Then he passed through the land of the Benjamites, but they did not find them.

Saul finds himself in a tough position. His father lost the donkeys and asked him to go look for them. Sounds simple, right? Nope. Instead, for three days Saul and the servant searched day and night and still could not find them.

Let me just say that this wasn't encouraging. Saul probably thought he was out of God's will. Searching and searching to no end would lead many to believe they were out of the will of the Father. There are seasons of life when we feel as if all we are doing is searching for lost donkeys. And many people today find themselves looking for things that were lost—peace, purpose, joy, healing, just to name a few. But God the Father had other plans for Saul. As they were on the journey, the Bible says the servant asked Saul to go see a prophet, and maybe the seer would help them find the animals. Of course, Saul said yes. Clearly when you look at the story, they had nothing to lose. Here's more of the story:

> Now the LORD had told Samuel in his ear the day before Saul came, saying, "Tomorrow about this time I will send you a man from the land of Benjamin, and you shall anoint

him commander over My people Israel, that he may save My
people from the hand of the Philistines; for I have looked
upon My people, because their cry has come to Me."

So when Samuel saw Saul, the LORD said to him, "There
he is, the man of whom I spoke to you. This one shall reign
over My people." Then Saul drew near to Samuel in the gate,
and said, "Please tell me, where is the seer's house?"

Samuel answered Saul and said, "I am the seer. Go up
before me to the high place, for you shall eat with me today;
and tomorrow I will let you go and will tell you all that is
in your heart. But as for your donkeys that were lost three
days ago, do not be anxious about them, for they have been
found. And on whom is all the desire of Israel? Is it not on
you and on all your father's house?"

1 Samuel 9:15–20 NKJV

This is amazing. Here is a picture of a young man who
is clearly lost after looking for donkeys for three long days.
Meanwhile, as Saul is searching, God is speaking to the
prophet Samuel and explaining that someone will be coming whom he needs to anoint.

Three Keys to Positioning Ourselves

Saul eventually found the prophet Samuel, who talked to him
about what the Lord had to say concerning the donkeys. I
find it wild that the prophet tells Samuel the donkeys are
okay and have been found, and that Samuel needs to trust
and to eat at his house. I believe this holds a prophetic key
for us. In fact, I see three keys in this story that will help
us position ourselves to hear God more clearly: (1) honor
authority, (2) eat at the prophet's house (value the prophetic

179

and what's being served), and (3) value the anointing. Let's look at each of these three keys more closely.

Key 1: Honor authority.

I cannot explain how powerful this first key is. Saul was searching for the animals because his father had asked him to. He was willing to go look for something that was lost, even though he didn't know where or understand why, because authority had told him to. I know many people who love the prophetic, but they are simply out of alignment because they don't honor authority. They don't go to a church, or if they do, they simply are not accountable to anyone, and there is no one speaking into their lives.

As a pastor, I often ask people at our church, "Who is your pastor?" I ask some people this knowing that they attend, but also understanding that they are not covered, because they are unaccountable to anyone and don't listen to what I have to say. As we learned earlier, spiritual fathering and mothering matters, and having accountability matters!

Too many times, I have looked at certain young people and have highlighted to them, "You have an authority issue. You don't need to fix it right this second, but you do need to realize that eventually you will have to deal with it if you are planning on moving forward with God." Our universities and colleges have taught a generation that "critical thinking" is a trait to be respected and will lead to knowledge and power. Yet honoring authority is everything, and we have to learn to listen to our fathers, even when we don't understand.

Key 2: Eat at the prophet's house (value the prophetic and what's being served).

The second key vital to positioning ourselves to hear God was demonstrated when Saul was told to come to the prophet's house and eat. This is amazing. Before he could ever find the donkeys, he needed to come and eat with the prophet. There is a truth we must learn here: We must value the prophetic. We have to be willing to "eat" what the Lord is saying. We cannot twist and manipulate prophecy to fit our unbelief.

I know a girl who was praying and asking God if she should marry a certain man. Despite her pastors and friends telling her this was not the guy, she repeatedly asked God for a sign. One day as she was driving, she saw the boyfriend's name on the side of a truck. Then she saw his name on a storefront sign. Despite God speaking to her in many ways that this was not the man for her, she believed the truck and the storefront sign instead.

Valuing the prophetic does not mean we ignore our leaders and pastors. It means we have to value the word coming forth, even when it doesn't fit in with our desires. Saul ate with the prophet; it didn't matter what he had thought would happen before.

Another truth we must learn from this is that we must be careful where and what we eat. You are where and what you eat. In this case, Saul ate from the prophet's house, and we know what happened. He became anointed and received promotion.

What you devour will dominate you. We were just reading about Saul's sudden anointing as king over Israel. However, later in this same Bible book, you will read that Saul didn't die honorably. His way became rough because of his choices. In 1 Samuel 28:3, we see Saul driving out all the spiritists and mediums in the land. Then he becomes afraid that the Philistines are closing in on him, and he doesn't feel as though God is with him. Samuel is dead, so Saul goes to a medium for help. God hijacks the demonic séance, so that this medium actually summons up Samuel! Coming back from the dead, Samuel talks to Saul:

> Then Samuel said: "So why do you ask me, seeing the LORD has departed from you and has become your enemy? And the LORD has done for Himself as He spoke by me. For the LORD has torn the kingdom out of your hand and given it to your neighbor, David. Because you did not obey the voice of the LORD nor execute His fierce wrath upon Amalek, therefore the LORD has done this thing to you this day. Moreover the LORD will also deliver Israel with you into the hand of the Philistines. And tomorrow you and your sons will be with me. The LORD will also deliver the army of Israel into the hand of the Philistines."
>
> Immediately Saul fell full length on the ground, and was dreadfully afraid because of the words of Samuel. And there was no strength in him, for he had eaten no food all day or all night.
>
> And the woman came to Saul and saw that he was severely troubled, and said to him, "Look, your maidservant has obeyed your voice, and I have put my life in my hands and heeded the words which you spoke to me. Now therefore, please, heed also the voice of your maidservant, and let me set a piece of bread before you; and eat, that you may have strength when you go on your way."
>
> But he refused and said, "I will not eat."
>
> So his servants, together with the woman, urged him; and he heeded their voice. Then he arose from the ground and sat on the bed. Now the woman had a fatted calf in the house, and she hastened to kill it. And she took flour and kneaded it, and baked unleavened bread from it. So she brought it before Saul and his servants, and they ate. Then they rose and went away that night.
>
> 1 Samuel 28:16–25 NKJV

That's a wrap. Saul ate from the prophet and became king over Israel. Later, he eats at the medium's and then kills himself the next day (see 1 Samuel 31).

Let me give you an unpopular opinion: You were never meant to "eat" the word of every prophet across the country. You were never meant to watch every church's livestream. Yes, I said it. It will be destructive for you!

Years ago, we could go to our church and the pastor would seek God and deliver a word each week for us. If we thought about going to any special services elsewhere, the pastor would help guide us about whether he thought it was a good idea. (I would always ask my pastor first about going.) Because just as Paul said, everything may be permissible, but not everything is always beneficial (see 1 Corinthians 10:23).

Jumping around from church to church, listening to every church's livestream—one preacher one day, an evangelist the next—you will start to think God is confused and crazy. You were never meant to listen to every person's livestream on the planet!

Think about it: Growing up, you were never meant to eat at every neighbor's house on your street. Sure, occasionally you ate dinner at a friend's house as a treat, but you ate most of your meals at home, with the family you belonged to. The same thing is true spiritually. God has put you in a spiritual family where you are fed, and you eat most of your meals there. Occasionally, it can be a blessing to be fed elsewhere, but home is where your health is. What you "eat" or consume spiritually is vital for your future and your positioning to hear God. Whom we hear from matters.

Key 3: Value the anointing.

Saul listened to his father and went to search for the donkeys. He went to the prophet for help, and then suddenly, after the meal they shared, the Bible says that Samuel opened a flask of oil and poured it on Saul's head. Instantly, suddenly, Saul went from a place of looking for lost donkeys to having oil poured on his head and being named king over Israel!

We must value the Holy Spirit. We must realize that there is a greater power and authority that God wants to have come upon us. There are many baptisms available for you—water baptism, but also baptism in fire and in the Holy Spirit (see Matthew 3:11). You cannot live in the encounter you had back in the 1990s. We must encounter God fresh today. There is a fresh fire available for you and me!

A Prophetic Word: "Get Ready"

If you have made it this far, you have done amazing! Clearly, you value the presence and power of God. Clearly, the prophetic is something you desire in a greater measure, and here is a final prophetic word for you. God is speaking to me so clearly, and I hear Him saying this:

Get ready—a "suddenly" is about to come upon your life. I am about to show you signs and wonders you have not seen before! This will be a year of suddenlies, and this will be a year of recovery.

Get ready—you are about to see your family come under My presence. I am about to show you My glory in a greater measure than you have ever known. You are stepping into a new season today! This will be a season of fulfilled promises and dreams restored.

Today, I am placing a new anointing upon you. You will be My awakeners in this next season, and the greatest harvest you have ever seen will enter the Kingdom!

184

Wow. *Thank You, Lord.* I feel God's presence so strongly as I write this. That word was for you! Write it down and read it over again. I believe today is the first day of forever. Get ready!

As you apply the principles in these pages to your life, get ready to be positioned to walk in a greater measure of authority and power. As you put the 10 prophetic values for today into practice, get ready to hear God's voice more frequently and more clearly than ever before.

Powerful Points about the Prophetic

- One final time, the 10 prophetic values we talked about in these pages are the value of integrity, the value of priority, the value of perseverance, the value of emotional health, the value of relationships, the value of loving the written Word of God, the value of endless hope, the value of knowing what we've been given, the value of our speech, and the value of generosity.

- Every single promise God has given us is conditional. Fulfilled promises are a result of prayer, faith and positioning. How we are positioned will determine our harvest!

- Standing on the Word of God and obeying His instructions about the way we should live will position us for hearing His voice.

- The Father wants to speak to us, and it is all about positioning. Too often, we don't create a safe space to learn to hear God.

- As we make room for God, He will make room for us. When we make room just to be and to listen to Him, then we will watch the "suddenlies" happen in our lives.

- Three prophetic keys from the story of Samuel anointing Saul will help us position ourselves to hear God more clearly: (1) honor authority, (2) eat at the prophet's house (value the prophetic and what's being served), and (3) value the anointing (see 1 Samuel 9).

- I cannot explain how powerful key 1, honor authority, is. I know many people who love the prophetic, but they are simply out of alignment because they don't honor authority. They are not accountable to anyone, and there is no one speaking into their lives.

- Key 2, eat at the prophet's house, means for us today that we have to be willing to "eat" what the Lord is saying, not twist or manipulate it to fit our own agenda. We have to value the prophetic and be careful where and what we eat spiritually.

- We must value the Holy Spirit and value the anointing, as key 3 tells us. We cannot live in past encounters; we must encounter God afresh today. There is a fresh fire available for you and me!

- As you apply the principles in these pages to your life, get ready to be positioned to walk in a greater measure of authority and power. As you put the 10 prophetic values for today into practice, get ready to hear God's voice more frequently and more clearly than ever before.

NOTES

Chapter 1 A Hearing Heart

1. See, for example, the Peshitta Holy Bible translation of this passage, available online at Bible Hub, https://biblehub.com/hpbt/1_kings/3.htm.

Chapter 2 Pure Children of God

1. Wikipedia, s.v. "2008 United States presidential election," last modified April 14, 2022, https://en.wikipedia.org/wiki/2008_United_States _presidential_election.

2. Oxford Learner's Dictionaries, s.v. "integrity," Oxford University Press, https://www.oxfordlearnersdictionaries.com/us/definition/english /integrity?q=integrity.

Chapter 3 The Discipline to Say No

1. The statistics in this list are taken from Pastor Jentezen Franklin's September 10, 2019, sermon "The Power of Distraction," available online at https://www.youtube.com/watch?v=WeOPaPcyPVA.

2. I'm quoting John Wimber to the best of my memory from his Signs and Wonders 101 course, which is also widely quoted by many Vineyard pastors and in numerous blogs.

Chapter 5 The Power of Peace

1. "SAMHSA releases 2020 National Survey on Drug Use and Health: Data show COVID's impact on nation's mental health, substance use," SAMHSA online (Substance Abuse and Mental Health Services Administration), October 26, 2021 (last updated April 6, 2022), https://www .samhsa.gov/newsroom/press-announcements/202110260320.

Chapter 7 Hearing with Confidence

1. To watch my "Supernatural Stories" segment that aired on Sid Roth's *It's Supernatural!*, visit https://www.youtube.com/watch?v=pC NfHxv_MVY.

Chapter 8 The Anchor of Hope

1. The Britannica Dictionary, s.v. "anchor," https://www.britannica .com/dictionary/anchor.

Chapter 9 Rediscovering the Kingdom

1. "Kathryn Kuhlman: 'We're Asking a Cupful; the Ocean Remains,'" YouTube, May 7, 2018, https://www.youtube.com/watch?v=IQKIPyO Dcdw.

2. Melissa Chan, "Here's How Winning the Lottery Makes You Miserable," *Time*, January 12, 2016, https://time.com/4176128/powerball -jackpot-lottery-winners/.

Chapter 10 The Power of Words

1. See, for example, the Worrell New Testament translation of this passage. This Bible version was published in 1904, but a 1980 Gospel Publishing House reprint is available.

James Levesque is an author, church planter and international speaker. He is also the founder and lead pastor of a network of Engaging Heaven churches across North America.

Pastor James and his wife, Debbie, are widely regarded among the young, emerging apostolic champions of revival and awakening in the United States and beyond. They are passionate about seeing lives transformed through Jesus Christ.

Pastor James's books *Revival Hunger: Finding Genuine Revival among Fluff and Hype* (Destiny Image, 2011) and *Fire: Preparing for the Next Great Holy Spirit Outpouring* (Chosen, 2019) challenge readers to awaken to the call of God for their lives and to surrender to the fullness of His glory in these last days.

Pastor James also hosts the popular daily podcast *Engage Heaven*. He is the host of various TV shows on Spirit-filled living, including *Breaking Through with James Levesque* and *Love Living Life* on the Christian Television Network (CTN).

Together, James and Debbie live in beautiful Clearwater, Florida, with their three wonderful children, Isaac, Luke and Amayah.

To find out more about James and his ministry, visit www.engagingheaven.com, or listen to his daily podcast. To invite James to speak, contact engagingheaven@gmail.com. You can also keep up with him online:

Facebook: www.facebook.com/JamesLevesque1
Twitter and Instagram: @James_Levesque

More from
James Levesque

The world has wandered so far from God that nothing short of awakening will reignite the fires of revival. Filled with powerful inspiration and real-life stories, this book shares twelve biblical principles that will unlock the passionate and faith-filled life you've longed for. The Kingdom is now; here are the secrets to taking it.

Fire!

Stay up to date on your favorite books and authors with our free e-newsletters. Sign up today at chosenbooks.com.

 facebook.com/chosenbooks

 @Chosen_Books

 @chosen_books